and the Path to Enlightenment

A Reiki and Shamanic Journal for Energy Healing Students, Practitioners and Teachers

Laura O'Neale

Published by Your Light Within LLC

Copyright ©2011 by Laura O'Neale
U.S. Copyright Office - Case No 1-603975211
All rights reserved

Requests for permission to record, photocopy, perform or reproduce any part of this book should be sent to
Laura@YourLightWithin.com

This book can be used as handout for Reiki Students and Teachers.

The author of this book does not dispense medical advice or prescribe the use of any technique as a form of treatment for physical or medical problems without the advice of a physician. Energy work such as Reiki is classified as Complementary Medicine, and does not substitute for or interfere with medical treatments. In the event you use any of the information in this book for yourself, which is your constitutional right, the author and publisher assume no responsibility for your actions.

Cover Design by Laura O'Neale and Ion (John) Bogdan Dragutescu

ISBN 978-0-578-08469-5

Published in the United States of America by
Your Light Within LLC

Printed in the United States of America

Will be also translated into Romanian and published in Romania.

With love and gratitude,
Reiki and the Path to Enlightenment
is dedicated to all my spiritual family.

Acknowledgments

From the bottom of my heart I acknowledge my grandparents, parents, spiritual teachers, friends, students, spiritual partners—who have contributed to my happiness, growing and learning process directly and indirectly, through sharing their love, teachings, support, requests for support, inspiration, and more. Love is the source of life, and needs to be acknowledged, nurtured and shared. Be blessed through eternity!

With love and gratitude, I give special thanks to:
Samantha Beathy, my first Reiki Teacher
Shaman Manin, my Spiritual Teacher
Bob Hickman, my Spiritual Consultant
All my Reiki students, clients and spiritual partners
Sue Bracey, for valuable insights
Hugh O'Neale, for valuable insights and especially, for being an amazing spiritual partner and true source of love
Ion (John) Bogdan Dragutescu, for graphics and cover design
Elisabeth Hallett, for line editing (author of *Stories of the Unborn Soul*)

Contents

Introduction	9
Taking Reiki Classes	**13**
Becoming a Reiki I practitioner	14
Becoming a Reiki II practitioner	23
Becoming a Reiki Master	37
The Reiki Initiations Transformed my Life	**45**
A spiritual trip to Sedona	45
Learning more through dreams, life experiences and Reiki practice	58
My new vision about romantic love	64
Reiki and Christianity	69
Steps Forward in Psychic Development	**73**
Shaman Manin – my "Shamama"	**79**
Teaching Reiki – a Transformational Soul Mission	**93**
What I've learned by teaching Reiki I	94
What I've learned by teaching Reiki II	104
What I've learned by teaching Reiki III	117
The more practice, the more lessons	127
A Spiritual Trip to Romania	**131**
A New Soul Mission	**153**

Our Reiki Family	**159**
Tools for Energy Healers:	**169**
Reminders for our inner healer	**169**
Reiki Student's Handout	**173**
Gifts from Stellar Beings, channeled by Shaman Manin	**197**
About the Author	**201**

Introduction

Beloved readers,

Thank you for your calling to read *Reiki and the Path to Enlightenment.*
This book is one of my journals. Each of my journals is a book for me, a book for you, and a book for life. We are one.

It doesn't matter what page of this book you will read. They are all filled with love for you. Take what inspires you from *Reiki and the Path to Enlightenment.*
Enjoy, feel and breathe this book.

As you breathe and read, your spirit learns. Then, you become. The word *become* is formed by *be* and *come.*
"*Come* to me and *be.*"—God said to me.

What is Reiki? What is Enlightenment? How can Reiki be useful on the path to Enlightenment?
These are questions you might ask yourself.

Reiki and the Path to Enlightenment gives simple answers through many insights I had throughout the years while healing myself, learning and teaching Reiki.

*

Enlightenment is an ongoing process, an inward journey. Our light within can shine when we break through the shell of unhealed old wounds, that feels like a heavy armor.
Then we stop identifying with our ego, stepping into Universal Consciousness.

We are all on this process of enlightening, or awakening. All of us are awakening, some sooner, and some later. The ones who do it earlier live longer in happiness, that's all!

This is what I've learned about the enlightenment process:
-We feel the need to heal ourselves and we take action. We realize that relationships are the key of our happiness. We are eager for completion, especially with our origins, our physical and spiritual parents.
Completion keys: "Forgive me. I love you. Thank you."
-We realize that after respect and love for physical and spiritual parents, comes respect and love of self*.
- Love of self gives the desire to heal self. When healing self, at the energetic level a heavy armor falls apart. Then, we can shine, we can be our light within, in other words, enlightened.
- The light gets brighter as we expand self toward *unity*.
- Unity comes through love and compassion.
- Ego, the part of us who says "I am better than you" becomes obedient.
- We realize that there is no need for suffering when there is no need for ego's manifested identity.
- Fear of death disappears when we know who we are, when we know our eternity.
- Ego becomes our servant. "I am here to serve" is what ego gets to say to *our spirit*.

Enlightenment means to be focused on light: the light of our spirit, the light of spirit.

*

Reiki is a path filled with light:
- It gives us the physical, emotional, mental and spiritual magic wands of healing
- It helps heal self
- It heals others through us, therefore it helps serve others
- It creates a powerful connection with people who are either receiving or giving Reiki healing sessions or initiations. As a result of this interaction, unity expands to the highest level: unity with people, unity with the spiritual guides of people.
- It comes from the same source as the Universal Consciousness, and therefore it brings infused knowledge and divine inspiration.
-Reiki distant healing, in particular, helps develop psychic abilities. The more our senses open, the more we can see and hear the love of God.

Reading about Reiki, as you believe it is true, you will want to know that it is true. For that, you will *become* a healer of body, mind and spirit.

Shamanic Practices include Energy Healing. Reiki is just one of the Energy Healing Modalities.

*

Reiki and the Path to Enlightenment is not only a book, but also a Reiki class handout if you so choose. Hand this book out, Energy Healing teachers.

Use this handout, Energy Healing students. "Handout" means that it is out-of-my-hands. It is yours to believe, re-create, update and become who you choose to be. We are co-creators with God.

Our creativity is the umbilical cord between us and the Creator. I invite you to use this book as inspiration and point of reference, and practice the way you are guided by spirit.

As we choose to be focused on spirit, we are one.

This book is also a gift for my teachers, so that the world knows how much soul, spirit and love they poured into me. Thank you through eternity!

The cover was designed in honor of Dr. Mikao Usui, the Japanese Buddhist who rediscovered Reiki and who spread its blessings in the world. While meditating, standing under a waterfall that was known to open the crown chakra, he suddenly felt the great Reiki energy at the top of his head, which led to the Reiki healing system.

The writing comes from my heart. It is not stylish, but profound and free. I did not write like that before Reiki, Shamanic Practices, and *you*... being *one* with you. I love you.
Enjoy!

In joy,
Laura and noi (in Romanian, my native language, "noi" means "we")

* Note: You can read more about completion, self-love, love and self-discovery in my book, *The Journey of the Colorful Stars*.

Taking Reiki Classes

After 33 years of life, I had finally fully understood and started to follow my destiny. I am here to live from the heart, to learn and teach through love, and to be a tool for spiritual healing in the hands of the Creator.

Reiki was presented to me as being a wonderful pathway. In divine time, I stepped into this life transforming chapter of my life. I was ready to *become* a healer of body, mind and spirit.

What really fascinated me about Reiki as a hands-on healing modality were the four different keys/symbols used to address energy imbalances at all levels: physical, emotional, mental and spiritual. Using all four keys, Reiki doesn't treat just the effect, but the root cause of anything.

To become a Reiki Master and have access to all four levels of healing, one has to take all Reiki levels. There are three levels, and for each one, the student is given by the teacher a Reiki attunement (initiation, empowering) that opens and aligns the energy centers to the new vibration. It takes up to five minutes for the Reiki Master to pass the attunement; however, it takes 21 days for the student's energy fields to align to the new level of vibration.

***

Becoming a Reiki I practitioner

What really amazed me was the definition of Reiki: ***Spiritually Guided Life Force Energy***. The two elements of the word Reiki are ***Rei***, meaning God, or Spiritual Guidance, and ***Ki***, meaning Life Force Energy. My life-changing dream that I had around the age of 19, in which a huge spiral of colorful stars was coming down from the Universe and entering in a Holy Cross, popped in my mind instantly. In that dream, the colorful stars represented the Life Force Energy. As a Christian, the Holy Cross was the symbol of my faith. Learning the definition of Reiki, in an instant my dream made even more sense as being the premonition of the spiritual path I was supposed to follow.

We were taught that Reiki is not religious but it is spiritual, and can be incorporated in everyone's religion. From the first five minutes of our Reiki class, I realized that Reiki will flow best through me as I am strengthening my faith. I was fascinated! My days and nights were so magic, my whole life shifted to a new dimension. "I truly am on my path!"

During the first Reiki level, we were given a Reiki symbol representing a tool for healing at the physical level. We were encouraged to do Reiki on ourselves, on plants, on the trees, the Earth, on animals, children, water and food.

We were taught that Reiki can't hurt, and Reiki Sessions can be complementary to any medical treatment, however, it doesn't substitute for any medical treatment.

We were also introduced to the major seven chakras - the major energy centers of the body:
Root (red/at the base of the spine)
Sacral (orange/belly button area)
Solar plexus (yellow/stomach area)
Heart (green/middle of chest)
Throat (blue/at throat)
Third eye (purple/forehead) and
Crown (white/top of head).

The seven main chakras

Since there are a lot of referrals to the chakras from now on in this book, under the "Reiki Student's Handbook" chapter, you can find a pretty detailed description of each one.

We were taught that there are over 100 chakras in our body, and the most powerful ones following the main seven chakras are:

-The palm chakras – connected with the heart. That confirmed my belief that healing and love are deeply connected.

-The feet chakras – connected with the root chakra. That explained for me the importance of walking barefoot on occasions. This simple act increases our life-force energy so much!

-The breasts chakras (for women) – this tells that breast feeding is so much more than it seems to be. The energy transfer between the mother and the child during nursing can't be substituted by any "formula."

*

After the first Reiki attunement, my hands started to tingle more often. Other parts of my body started too— my shoulders, my feet, the tips of my fingers, my face; sometimes it felt as if currents of electricity were running through me for a few minutes at a time, out of the blue. As the energy started to go up the spine, from root to crown, my body, mind and spirit were going through a lot of changes. It takes about three days for each chakra to align to the new level of energy.

In the first three days, I woke up earlier, full of life and energy; everything was possible! I felt safe and secure, which made sense since the root chakra—the energy center that is in charge of safety and security—was being balanced. The following few days, my enthusiasm for everything and everyone around me was absolutely amazing, which also made sense since the sacral chakra, which is in charge of the quality of our relationships, was being balanced. Every night I was burning incense sticks, drawing the Reiki symbol on my palms, on my body, on each wall and on my bed before I went to sleep. I studied a little bit about gemstones and got a set of stones for my chakras. Sometimes I would meditate with them, charge them with Reiki and then place them under the mattress or under the pillow overnight. Gemstones are very special to me.

The Reiki principles, provided and discussed as part of the Reiki I class, printed on our Reiki Certificates, were now placed in a few places in my studio and at work. They were now my new affirmation, and their wisdom was liberating:

REIKI PRINCIPLES

- Just for Today -
I will trust,
I will be at peace,
I will do my work honestly,
I will accept my many blessings,
I will show Gratitude to every living thing,
And I will respect the rights of ALL CREATION.

While my heart chakra, which is in charge of the depth of our love, was being balanced, a very distinct feeling of compassion and love for everyone in my life, and particularly for my very old grandmother, Mama Nana, was leading my days. It was as if a window was cleaned for me to see the beauty outside… I spent hours and hours imagining how I am going to visit Romania—my home country, and take good care of my grandmother, who at the time was blind, unable to walk, spending her days in bed, being totally dependent on my mother. I wanted to be there and comb her hair, wash her body, massage her, do Reiki on her.

Unity comes through love and compassion

About a week later, while my crown chakra, which is basically the gateway to the Divine, was being balanced, for the first time in my life I felt that I can accept in peace what can't be done, and do my best for what can be done, with the will of God.

*

One day I burned my fingers with the ironing machine. The pain was sharp, but after a few minutes I decided to use Reiki. With my eyes closed, I imagined that I'm breathing in Reiki healing light through my crown chakra and breathing it out through my hands, from inside out into my fingers. In a matter of seconds, the pain disappeared. The burn was there, but it didn't look too bad, and it didn't hurt at all.

*

In one of my dreams, I was drawing the "physical body" Reiki symbol made of light, as it was coming out of my hands. After that dream, I started to imagine that as being real.

*

Once I was sitting on the edge of a fountain where many people gathered. All of a sudden, an idea popped in my mind: to draw the Reiki symbol in the water, for all people who will watch or touch the water to receive the Reiki blessing. The idea came with a specific kind of joy—spiritual joy. As we learn to interpret our body's signals, we learn to distinguish our own thoughts from our guidance. With regard to Reiki, that moment unfolded my first guidance about being a channel for healing. It was a blissful moment.

*

On a Sunday morning, I was reading in a park, on a bench. A family came close and their child was playing in the grass. He found a little colorful stone and was looking at it with joy and amazement. It reminded me of my childhood, when I used to do the very same thing—to enjoy the colorful stones found in the sand. With a big smile on my face I pulled one of my gem stones out of my crystal bag, charged it with the Reiki energy in my palms for a few minutes and then gave it to him. The same kind of joy felt not long ago filled my heart. It seemed like I was guided and shown ways to do Reiki by a higher power. I was fascinated and a sense of fulfillment made my heart sing.

*

There were many huge old trees along the sidewalk on my way to work. Every night, on my way back home, I would stop and touch one of the oldest trees, and draw the Reiki symbol on its bark. A deeper knowing of oneness with nature awakened in my heart. The light flowing through me was the light flowing through the tree… in my imagination, the tree was even more of a healer than me —its channels were wide and clean—no barriers, no obstacles, no doing… just being.

"What is seen, of any object, a tree, an animal, a stone, a man is only a part of that tree, animal, stone, or man. There is a force which for a time binds such objects together in the form you see them. This ever-acting, ever-varying force, which lies behind and, in a sense, creates all forms of matter we call Spirit." - Prentice Mulford - Thoughts are Things

*

A dear Reiki classmate went to a restaurant for dinner with a group of friends. She drew the Reiki symbol over her plate. Later, everyone except her became sick from the food. She had many food allergies and could have been way more affected than any of her friends, but she was in perfect shape. Her story amazed me and also invited me to use Reiki all the time, and create a new context for everything I was doing.

*

Being a student at the massage school, where people are hands-on healing oriented, gave me a lot of opportunities to practice Reiki. The sessions were pretty amazing, all my classmates felt a lot of heat and a deep feeling of love and peace surrounded them during the sessions. Every day was a gift and a miracle.

*

One of my most beloved friends came over to my place. She had been fighting a cold for about two weeks. I gave her a long Reiki session, and let all my love for her flow through me, prayed and visualized her being healthy and full of life and joy. After about a half hour, she felt so much better, and then she finally slept well the entire night. It made me so happy to hear that, and I saw once more how much being present and loving, and caring deeply, is the most important healing tool on Earth.

*

The nasty part was that my ego played big trying to take over: I loved to believe that I'm the healer, and I do miracles, therefore I'm special. Reiki teachings were very clear about the fact that a Reiki practitioner is a channel of energy, that *we give through us, not from us*, that we are facilitating healing, not doing healing.
"Be humble, Laura. Ego hurts and it doesn't let you see many things," I told myself; easy to say, hard to do.

Until we get to the roots of our behavior and attitudes, knowing about our weaknesses isn't enough. Trying to control is like dusting in a dark room. I'm stressing this because it is a very common challenge on the pathway of a healer and/or psychic.

It's a long learning process, but moreover, a deep internal transformation through healing.

Only when we're healed and when we truly love ourselves, we lose our need to prove ourselves. Reiki definitely is a great self-healing tool, and it takes a lot of time and attention, so I am encouraging everyone to get the tools and look within and do the work, rather than rely only on outside support.

Ego may never stop playing games, but it happens less and less as we love ourselves more and more. Self love comes with the liberation from guilt, shame, fear, anger, with the healing of our emotional traumas and ultimately by following our soul-mission.

***

Becoming a Reiki II practitioner

The time for emotional healing had come. We were given tools for that. It was amazing how all my past traumas were terrified by being now threatened, and came up from the past to give me a really awful episode of misery and pain, right before the Reiki II attunement. I couldn't even breathe with anxiety and sadness. It took me over completely for hours.

We were given a warning that emotional traumas will come up, but now we have the tools to heal them. We were taught to do healing on our Master Guides and Spiritual Guides, who would then support us through the process of self-healing. We were also given the tools for distant healing—for the past, the present and the future. We were highly encouraged to take our time and address all our past traumatic events with Reiki.

Being committed to become a healer comes with the obligation of self-healing.

Why is this affirmation true: while serving others, their pain would trigger the healer's pain, and all of a sudden the healer finds himself/herself being concerned with his/her own persona, and unable to help anyone else.

*

Offering Reiki light to my spirit guides

So I went home and did Reiki on Jesus's feet. Tears were falling down my face, while asking Jesus to receive my offering of light.

My emotional traumas were there, and my pain was so intense, it made me kneel in front of Jesus's icon, begging for forgiveness, begging for help. The session gave me enough peace to be able to go to sleep and rest well the whole night, having no dreams or anxiety. I had doubts, though, that the Reiki session had any effect. "Who am I to be given this gift?" It was the gift I had wanted for so long, yet still didn't truly believe it was given to me....

We tend to be comfortable with who we know ourselves to be, and resist change even when that's all we ever wanted. So my emotional traumas were still there, and as the day went on, the anxiety became so intense that I didn't dare even to think about them in detail, being afraid that I'll just stir up the fire even more.

The second night I did Reiki on my Spiritual Guides, using the Native American poster near my bed. The poster depicts four spiritual guides, bringing energy from the four directions. I sent the Reiki symbols to each of the guides, sent them light and love, and prayed for the healing of any emotional traumas they had while being incarnated. Then I meditated on the poster for a long time, sending light through my eyes to its center point. This second session also made me feel better and helped me find enough peace for a good night's sleep.

In my dream, I was dancing in the middle of a circle of fire, with bare feet on the dirt. At some point, I heard a gunshot and people screaming. Then I saw an old Native American Shaman chanting. It was like a ceremonial song... Aaaaa-Oooooo-Aaaaa-Oooo.... And then a voice was saying, "The captain killed the shaman's son in 1..83." I woke up.

Was the dream born in my imagination or was it a gift from my spiritual guides showing me where my Reiki session went? Was the Native American shaman one of my Spiritual Guides? Did he have a son who was shot in a battle? Did he receive my Reiki healing session and healed his pain for the loss of his son? I wanted to believe that this was the truth, but still had doubts about it till two years later when the shaman showed up in a mediumship session and thanked me for sending him light. (He confirmed then that his son was shot and that the healing sent by me addressed not only that, but many other wounds. He said that a lot of his people were killed that day.)

The third day was better but anxiety still took over from time to time. My plan was to do Reiki on my Spiritual Guides one more time, before starting to address my own emotional traumas from the past. And indeed, after the third session—this time on the soul of my first esoteric teacher, who had passed away about 13 years before—at night I had a dream that gave me the key of all my suffering. In my dream, my question was: *"Who was hurt?"* the answer came, deep in my heart: *"Ego."* I woke up right away and wrote down the short and on point dialog with my Spiritual Guides. Yes, it is that simple:

Our ego is the one who suffers. Our soul is always whole, perfect and complete. Therefore, all suffering is nothing but delusion.

This dream was liberating. However, as always, knowing is not enough. "Am I wrong for suffering? It wasn't fair!" I was arguing in vain.... Thank God, though, I really felt that I have no choice but to get to the bottom of things and take the time to heal my wounds.

Healing emotional wounds from my past

In the morning, I took a piece of paper and wrote down the first emotional trauma that I wanted to address: the first sexual abuse experienced as a still innocent youth. "I want to heal all my suffering related to this story, today, right now!"

I drew the Reiki symbols on my palms and on the piece of paper, then prayed and started my first self distant healing session. "Detach!" I told myself. With my eyes closed, I visualized myself being made of light and giving a Reiki session to a fifteen-year-old girl, who was me, in the past. I visualized "the young girl" sitting on a chair, and gave her a Reiki session, keeping my hands of light above each chakra, from crown to root, for a few minutes each. The Reiki Energy was blocked, though; it was coming out my luminous hands and floating around the young "me." The anxiety was still present and didn't seem to go away. The fear of failure started to creep in.

"What if I'm not going to be healed? What else can I do? I can't stand it anymore!" So I didn't give up, even though the temptation to do so was obvious. All of a sudden, my luminous body—the healer sent in my past—asked the young me: "Why do you feel all of this pain?" "Because I wonder how did he dare; because that's not fair; because I don't deserve that; because I am angry for not knowing how to defend myself..." "Ok, who suffered your *soul*, or your *ego*?" There was no way for me not to see the answer, especially after my dream "Ego suffered..." "Indeed... all of these arguments about what's not fair and what's not right are manifestations of your lack of acceptance for what you're supposed to go through.

You're alive, healthy, and on a spiritual path. Without this rough event, maybe you would never have gotten to follow your spiritual path. God knows better. *Give up your pain, God loves you.*"

In an instant, I visualized how all the light I'd been sending to the fifteen-year-old me was finally received... and a heavy burden like a metallic armor broke into pieces, falling apart. "But back then I didn't know that...." Ego still tried to defend. Listening to myself in the moment, I finally understood that by wanting to know and understand why things happen, in order to accept them, I'm holding onto the seeds of all suffering, and moreover, I do not trust God.

Trusting God means accepting things that happen to us even before understanding why they happened. The other way around faces the failure of understanding all the time, and as a result, we suffer.

There is no need for suffering when there is no need for ego's manifested identity. Being tuned into my spiritual essence, I see that the traumatic event in my past actually made me want to heal myself and develop myself as a healer.
Now I also know about karmic debts, and understand that I might have been inconsiderate, taking sexual advantage of someone in a previous life. Now I also see how my experience, and especially my self-healing, makes it possible for me to help other people heal their similar emotional traumas. But back then, I didn't know.... And only because of that, my life was haunted by pain for so many years. Hard lesson, should I never forget!

Trust God, do your best, but accept what you cannot change; there is a reason for everything, whether or not it's going to ever be revealed to you.

The next thing for me to do was to forgive him, my aggressor. "God, please help me forgive him forever, God, please release him of his karmic debts created by his behavior. God, please help him be humble in front of you, please help him be a good man." My hands of light went around him creating a cocoon of light. By forgiving him, I was liberated from a chain of negative energy created by my resistance against him as well as my own pain.

"Forgiveness is a gift you give to yourself. Genuine forgiveness does not happen by accident or with the passage of time. It is a conscious and deliberate choice"
- Rod Terry: the author of Hope Chest - A Treasure of Spiritual Keepsakes

At the end of the session, I gave the young me a hug and came back to *here and now*. My first self-healing Reiki session ended successfully, after more than an hour. Getting out of it, I was dizzy, but so peaceful and light, like a feather.
Looking back, it occurred to me that my luminous body—the healer sent in my past—was my higher self, my light within.

We all have a light within. We all have a healer within. We all have all of these miracles available to us. We just have to have faith, and let God lead our way.

*

28

This first successful self-healing session gave me the courage to continue addressing many other traumas from my past. For the following two weeks, I focused only on myself, doing distant healing every morning for about 45 minutes. It was really important for me to face all my unpleasant memories and wipe them all out. "I want to be the one stirring the fire up in a safe environment, rather than wait for life situations to do so." Having the key of all my suffering, it was actually much easier than I thought. To my surprise, my first self-healing session went through many other events following the date of the addressed event.

If you can only give up your fear, and all ego's games and tricks, your spirit then finds so many ways to simply fly higher and higher, and attain its mission.

All the pain I was going through in life helped me learn about healing, compassion, love, understanding, acceptance; these are tools for spiritual teaching, tools that are now helping many others liberate themselves.

"View every personal crisis as an opportunity for spiritual growth." - Rod Terry: the author of Hope Chest - A Treasure of Spiritual Keepsakes

Distant healing on my dear father

Feeling so much stronger, and seeing such good results, I felt ready to do distant healing on my family and friends. It's an ethical rule to ask for permission. How would I have dared to even ask without feeling the benefits of Reiki on myself first, especially when it comes to something so "untouchable" as distant healing?

The first person I've done a distant Reiki session on was my father.

After preparing a sacred space with lighted candles, unplugged phone and dim light, I sat comfortably and drew the Reiki symbols on my hands and on his photo. Then, with my eyes closed and my father's photo between my hands, I visualized him lying on his bed, and my luminous body doing Reiki on him. My palms were hot and tingling. My hands of light were placed on each of his seven chakras, one by one, for about two minutes each. Praying for his health and peace of mind connected me with my dear father in a very profound way. It was almost like I could feel the texture of his hair, the sweat on his forehead, his energy, his breathing, his nurturing, fatherly presence. I missed him, and tears were falling down my face…. "I love you so much, Daddy"…it was so real, it gave me a new perspective:

Practicing Reiki distant healing we can travel through time and space.

As my father's seven chakras were charged, I placed my hands of light on his pelvis, for his arthritis, but my luminous hands kept moving against my will on his heart. At some point my luminous body stepped back and sent him a light bolt of Reiki energy, in his entire aura. At the end of the session, I gave him a hug, and then came back to "here and now." Looking back, I noticed how powerfully my love for him allowed me to stay focused and allowed the energy to flow freely through me. However, I wasn't detached enough.

Finding the balance between being loving and being detached is one of the most important lessons to be learned by a healer.

After that session, I can't express my gratitude for having Reiki in my life as a tool of connection with my dear family back home in Romania.

Was the distance attracting Reiki as a tool for connection in my life, or was my spiritual pathway attracting the distance as a tool for growth?

A few days later I called my father and asked if he felt anything. His first reaction was to doubt it, since his expectations about Reiki were not well defined. He first said, "What do you expect, I have serious health problems." I explained that my expectations are not to hear that he's now free of arthritis, and asked him if he felt relaxed and peaceful. He said that indeed, he felt very relaxed and sleepy. In fact he couldn't get back to work on his project that day. He also told me that he was recently found to have a heart issue, which I didn't know about before the Reiki session, and that explained why my luminous hands were moving on his chest. It wasn't me knowing what was needed. It was the Spiritually Guided Life Force Energy at work.

*

In that period of time, basically my distant healing sessions were substituting for my regular meditation time. Later on I came back to my meditation ritual, and occasionally on weekends I would meditate in different ways, do distant healing on a family member or friend from Romania, pray, do yoga, for about 45 minutes each, and so it would be 2:00 p.m. in the afternoon when I would finally "start" the day.

*

Hands on emotional healing

While giving a Reiki session to a good friend, she first felt heat going down her spine, from crown to root. As my hands were going down, above her body, she knew where I was, with her eyes closed.
When my hands got above her sacral area, something felt different—more energy was flowing through me into her body, so I stopped there for a few minutes. Soon she had an emotional release that lasted for about ten minutes. I didn't ask her anything, just encouraged her to let it all go, while giving her all my love. At the end she felt so much better—she completely shifted to a state of profound peace.

*

Having amazing friends who believed in what I was doing, and being a student at the massage school, gave me plenty of opportunities to practice Reiki at least five times a week, sometimes even three times more. The journey was fascinating. Every time was different, every time something unexpected happened, teaching me that the Life Force Energy was indeed Spiritually Guided, and showing me and the person I was practicing on that the Reiki Energy knows so much more than I do. All I had to do was to open my heart and love genuinely every person I was doing Reiki on. The energy was flowing as needed, not more and not less.

Some of my friends who were in great shape didn't feel much, simply because Reiki energy would not flow for show… if it wasn't needed, it didn't flow.

*

Opened new doors

It was a wonderful Sunday afternoon when I discovered the Meridian Hill Park. It was so beautiful! The architecture made me feel like I was in a different world, an ancient castle.
I was studying, sitting down on a blanket under a tree, when I started to hear people playing drums. It was amazing! I felt so much joy in my heart, and followed the sound. I saw a big circle of drummers playing. They were so fascinating to me! Something ancient awoke in my heart…. Were they memories from another life, in an African tribe? I felt like I missed it, not like I just discovered it. With my eyes closed, letting it all in, I was in trance…. At some point I saw an elder Rastafarian brother, making fire. He looked familiar too…. "Where did we meet?" I asked myself. The feeling was out of this world….

Getting into the drum circle, it felt like I'd always belonged there, and played drums with them, and danced, and made the fire with my new elder friend, Ra. At the end, I invited Ra over for tea. It wasn't usual for me to trust and feel so comfortable with someone I just met. We had a two-hour amazing spiritual conversation. He was a healer and yogi, and the son of a clairvoyant woman.

At some point I asked him if he'd let me practice Reiki on him, and he said yes. My hands were tingling above his head and forehead, when a thought came into my mind: "I met Ra during Jesus's time." Then, later, while still doing Reiki on him, another message came to me: "He was the blind man Jesus healed." I got goose bumps, but didn't say anything to him. Was that true? "Maybe I'll never know, but there is a vibration matching the blind man from Jesus's times and a message for me about it," I thought.

I noticed that this message, that came while doing Reiki, *felt* different than my usual thoughts.

A few weeks later, Ra and I met again and had another long spiritual conversation. "We all have so much in common! As I study the human body—anatomy and physiology—I see that even more. We all have in common our bodies, God's perfect creation! I wish that people of all races could see how much we're all the same," I said.

"Yes, but we have these two eyes that are fooling us sometimes," he responded. "If you are blind, only love can lead your way. You don't know how the one who gives you something looks, you don't judge or evaluate people, you just pray, and receive with gratitude. You let the love flow freely through you, you believe that there is always love in the Universe for you, and that is a miracle." Wow, how did he know that? How can someone have such a deep understanding of a life experience they never had? Ra isn't blind... but what he just said matched the message I'd received during our first meeting. Wow! If that's true, is it also true that I lived during Jesus's times? "Did I meet Him?"...

—

34

At that point I couldn't keep it to myself and told Ra about the message gotten about him. "It could be," he said.

We concluded that, just as the blind man healed by Jesus, he represents the witness of miracles. I felt that I'm getting close to the day of living my own miracle.

*

Soon after that, while in the park again, I met Dawn, a beautiful young woman who had a little five-year-old beautiful daughter.
A week later we all went together to a spiritual event, and the little girl, Kaiya, went on the stage in the middle of the show and danced while the drummers were playing, without any barriers. "Kaiya *is the show*," I said. She had the purity of soul that we're striving to get back to, as mature people, through spiritual practices. Ra said:

We're coming down on Earth to lose ourselves and see if we can make it back

That night I met more amazing people... it seemed to me that the more I was going forward on a healer's pathway, the more doors started to open—it was like discovering a parallel world, a new dimension of life. Spirituality and healing were not new to me, though, but what was new was the free and open sharing with people, that made it real and attracted a new reality into my experience.

*

One day I met a guy in a coffee shop and had a wonderful conversation about healing arts and spiritual development. At some point he asked me: "Do you think any miracle could happen for the ones who are not open toward spiritual evolution?" I never thought about it but a message came in my mind: "There is a miracle in every cell of our bodies—we are a miracle! Yes, miracles always happen, all the time, for all of us, but when it comes to the miracle of spiritual awareness, everyone has a choice, and even God accepts that."

Inspiration seemed to shift to a different level... it felt as teamwork between my own being and other beings.... Were my spiritual guides talking through me sometimes or giving me messages? Was it the new, healed me? Was it because while letting the Reiki Energy flow through me, the door to the Universal Consciousness also opens?

One step at a time, I was discovering essential secrets of the Universe.

The Healing Force and the Universal Consciousness are flowing together, they are one!

***

Becoming a Reiki Master

During the Reiki III class, we were given the tools for Spiritual Healing (healing of the karmic causes of any disease). We were taught that sometimes it is too late to heal the physical body, and people would still die, but doing Reiki on them would still help heal them at the soul level.

Later on I understood that Reiki is much more than a tool for healing at all levels, it is a tool for Enlightenment.

We all have a light within, a spark of God. Letting our light shine requires healing at all levels, requires karmic healing.

We shared our experiences and self-healing, and just telling my Reiki group about my emotional healing sessions, all of a sudden I was again caught in a last anxiety attack. In that moment it seemed to me that all self-healing that occurred so far peeled off just a layer of the "onion"… but then I realized that I was healed way more profoundly than I thought. My last episode of anxiety was simply a reminiscence of the habit of being anxious about my past, a test, and the proof of my feeling safe with my Reiki Master, to the point where I've released the last drop of suppression.

We were given a summary of the four symbols. We were reminded that Reiki is not a religion but is spiritual in nature and therefore we can incorporate it in any religion. We were taught to place the four Reiki symbols on our walls:

physical healing on the North wall, *emotional healing* on the West wall, *mental/distant healing* on the East wall, and *spiritual healing* on the South wall.

During the Reiki III attunement, I had a profound feeling of oneness with my teacher and everyone else in the room. One of my friends who is a clairvoyant was there and gracefully accepted to look and see what happens during the attunement. She saw my teacher's aura and my aura merged the entire time. She saw white light going down my spine through all my chakras. A spirit guide was with me the entire time.

My friend's presence helped me understand that even if I'll never become a clairvoyant, we are *one*, and whatever I can't do, someone else can. *Teamwork for a common higher purpose is the way.* Ever since, I became willing to ask for help, both from other people and from Spirit Guides. I understood that trying to prove what I've done by myself only limits the results.

My relationship with Divinity transformed into an ongoing partnership. "God is healing through me whatever should be healed. I respect God's will and fully accept as much as God wants to be healed. I am a tool in God's hands. No attachment to results, no emotions, just love, faith, serenity, acceptance and light!"

*

As I got home at night, Ra came by to see me unexpectedly.

It really seemed to me that he was meant to be the first person in my life to talk to and spend a couple of hours with after my Reiki Master initiation. Becoming a Reiki Master was still a miracle for me, and so Ra really was the witness of my miracle.

*

Shifting my energy more and more

For the next few days, my body was tingling so intensely and so often, it was almost painful, especially my hands and the top of my head. It felt like someone was piercing into my crown chakra. I haven't experienced any anxiety anymore—it was peaceful and powerful. Doors opened for me in many ways—meeting amazing new people, finding valuable information, receiving great news from friends and family, getting many opportunities to practice Reiki on people. It felt like I was breathing a new air. The vibration, yes, this is what was different. I could almost feel it at the physical level. My meditations were profound and my mind was clear like a blue sky. What a miracle!

*

The favorite motivational quote provided in the Reiki materials was printed out on paper and placed in many places around my studio and on my keyboard in the office as well:

In the infinity of life where I am, all is perfect, whole and complete, I am always divinely protected and guided.
All is well in my world.
(Louise L. Hay – You Can Heal Your Life)

Some more self-healing was to be done

One night I did Reiki for the soul of my unborn child. If I had given birth to that child, he or she would have been twelve years old. I sent a lot of light, and spun the Reiki symbol into the soul's globe of light, and held the globe between my palms for a while as if it were a baby dove. A feeling of pure love filled my heart. I thanked the spirit of my unborn baby for teaching me a lesson about humanity, and a little angel came into my mind… it would have been a girl, and she was now the angel. Tears were falling down my face, but at the end, it was so much peace and completion… Thank you, angel!

During the same session, I then saw myself in a tub with water and many white roses floating on the water. Angels were pouring light into the water. The roses had light in their center. They were pure, and so I became, pure and filled with light, washing away, letting go all the guilt, misery, sorrow, sadness, and shame... Purity and light were my new costumes now, leaving behind not only that event, but any other that took my purity away in the past.

I encourage any woman who has experienced abortion, miscarriage, sexual abuse, blame, shame or any pelvic disease or breast disease, to take a bath in a tub filled with water and white beautiful roses, and ask for forgiveness, healing and peace. You don't have to know Reiki in order to do that. Your intention has power.

You will come out of the tub pure and filled with light, ready to embrace a new chapter of your life, one filled with joy and love, and infinite hope.

Enlightenment is a direct result of self-healing. Our wounds are a heavy metallic armor. As the armor breaks, our light within can shine.

*

We are being helped, to help

It was a Sunday afternoon, and I was tired after a long busy week at work, followed by a long weekend at the massage school. A headache and a general state of weakness took me over. Yes, I did have self-healing tools, but didn't find the strength to use them. I might have missed being a baby, and being taken care of. But here she comes, a massage schoolmate whom I've done Reiki on before, asking me for another session.

She had a sprain in her ankle and couldn't walk well for a long time. Being so tired, my first impulse was to say no, but instead I just asked her to give me a few minutes. "This is not fair, I need some help and care myself," I thought. Deep in my heart, though, I heard: "She was sent to you, you can't say no." Here was the battle between being in need and being of service. Thinking that "it's not fair to be asked for anything"—that was a typical ego based attitude. At that point I knew that, accepted where I was, and then accepted God's will—to be of service.

A few minutes after the session started, everything shifted. Focusing on the Reiki symbols, focusing on light, praying for her highest good, all of that together was such a blessing!
My breathing changed, a state of profound peace surrounded me, and all of a sudden I felt so relaxed, energized, and moreover, so loved, loved by God!

Opening my eyes for a second, I saw her smile—she was blissful too. My hands were warm and tingling, and the Reiki Energy was flowing freely. It was much needed and very well received. At the end of the session, we were both in great shape. A week later I found that her condition improved tremendously after that session. My lesson:

If we can only give up our needs and accept God's will for us, everyone wins. Otherwise, we are blocking the free flow of energy.

*

Distant healing and telepathy

Geny, one of my best friends from Romania, asked me for a distant healing session. It was a great experience. Our connection has been very powerful, we love each other so much, it was hard to stay detached. I missed her a lot at that point, and at the end of the session, to fully come back I had to use the Raku—the Reiki symbol that's normally used only for the purpose of completing a Reiki attunement, disconnecting the teacher's and student's auras.

It was amazing how accurate the visualization was during the session—talking with her later, we found that by the time I kept my hands on her feet and it felt cold, she actually had cold feet.
She felt a lot of heat and afterwards had an amazing day.

She told me that she perceived my energy as the energy of someone in love. I liked that and connected it with a very similar statement of one of my massage school classmates: "While you were doing Reiki on me, I felt much loved." These two experiences inspired me to create a new definition of Reiki:

Reiki is divine love flowing through the veins of the healer

*

The following day, Geny's friend wanted to experience a distant healing session too. I only had a photo of him with her, and did Reiki on the photo focusing on him. Later on, though, Geny asked me if I did Reiki on her again, since she felt a lot of heat. Wow, amazing, Reiki worked beyond my conscious intent... Geny actually very much needed the session right at that moment, and she had received it.

Later on, during my trip to Romania, both of them became Reiki Masters, to my absolute delight. It is an indescribable feeling of joy and fulfillment when great friends connect even more powerfully by creating a connection at the spiritual level.

*

The true miracle is in each of us

I am so grateful to my Reiki Teacher! She is a young and gorgeous woman, truly beautiful from inside out.

Her commitment to her spiritual pathway, and the sharing of her continuous spiritual growth, step by step, were paramount in building students' confidence. A teacher born with all spiritual gifts already opened wouldn't have given me so much confidence. My Reiki Teacher helped me realize that the true miracle is in each of us, waiting to be awakened. The Reiki training transformed my life. My teacher passed along to me and my classmates the Reiki key, a miraculous one. It was not enough, however, to have such a key in my pocket. I had to be willing to use it. But from that point on, it was up to me.

A Reiki Master is a tool in the hands of the Divine. It is not the person who gives the Reiki initiations, but a higher power. The Reiki Master simply passes the attunement/initiation. He/She doesn't have to be the most powerful healer alive on Earth, but simply someone with a pure heart, who is committed to her/his spiritual pathway, to their teachings, to the highest good of the world and of our planet.

Purity, love, joy, enthusiasm, commitment, simplicity, these are core values for a healer and teacher. I love my Reiki Teacher, acknowledge her, respect her and thank her for sharing the Reiki light, for making it possible for me and for so many others to become Reiki Masters.

Everything is possible where wisdom and love shine.

The Reiki Initiations Transformed my Life

A spiritual trip to Sedona

One of my dreams about America was to visit Sedona, where, as healers are saying, it's a special place of God, filled with natural energy vortexes. Many people told me how peaceful and connected they were there. Toward the end of my Reiki Master 21 day attunement process, I started to seriously consider spending a few days there. The thought came with excitement and no doubts, despite the fact that the cost associated with the trip would have exceeded my budget. It was meant to be, though, so the Universe helped me get the best offer to a hotel there, plus, I had exactly enough mileage accumulated to qualify for a free plane ticket. It was a real Reiki training "graduation gift."

While at my gate in the San Francisco airport, waiting for my connecting flight, I was reading *Trails*, by Rajeev Kasat. It was so fascinating to me, I completely lost track of time. I didn't hear any announcements, hadn't seen people boarding, missed my flight and realized that not after five minutes, but after 40 minutes....

While waiting for the next flight I met an amazing person who has been doing healing and spiritual counseling for 30 years.

Knowing that everything happens for a reason, I was open to hear and learn from him something perhaps very much needed at that point on my journey. He pointed out the importance of being flexible, of being detached, of not waiting for miracles to happen but rather allowing miracles to happen in one's life.

"We don't attract what we want, we attract what we are. Whatever we attract in our lives is in harmony with the average of our emotions and thoughts." -- Esther and Jerry Hicks (the Teachings of Abraham)

We were talking about my recent understanding about destiny: "When I felt in me and shared the possibility of being a healer of body, mind and spirit, actually I remembered who I am, I allowed myself to be who I really am. Re-entering in my chart, I started to live a purpose driven life."

He told me his story, his spiritual journey, and gave me hope seeing his huge progress along his life.

The conversation with this wonderful person set the tone of my spiritual retreat: "allow miracles to happen.... purpose driven life."

The ultimate evidence that miracles exist is simply the fact that we are.

*

When I got to Phoenix, it was already dark outside. It was the first time when, going by myself to a new place, I had to rent a car and hit the roads that late.

It was a two-hour trip to Sedona. Before I left the airport, I invited my Native American Spiritual Guides to enjoy being there and to guide me during my journey there.

At some point I wasn't even sure anymore if I was going in the right direction or not. It was in the middle of nowhere, and for more than twenty minutes I'd seen no cars, no houses, no lights...it wasn't scary though, but peaceful.... *a new feeling of freedom through guidance* surrounded me. It was a really good feeling. Eventually I got to the hotel. My dreams were very vivid and colorful that night, and my sleep really good and relaxing. In the morning, I opened the blinds and.... Wow... a huge red rock was right there, in front of my eyes.... It was magical!

By inviting divine guidance, we choose freedom from the fear generated by not being in control.

*

For three days, I went back and forth from one Energy Vortex to another, prayed, meditated and relaxed.

At the Bell Rock Energy Vortex, I felt tingling in my feet and my crown chakra, and a profound feeling of peace. While walking around the Vortex Area, at some point I was guided to sit down. I did, and soon after, felt a huge amount of energy flowing through my hands, through my crown, and through my heart. With my eyes closed, I saw many vortexes of light spinning all over around me. It was a unique visualization experience.

Then, with my eyes opened, I gazed at a far away red rock till I started to see white light around the whole rock formation—the aura of the red rocks.... God, it was so beautiful!

I closed my eyes again and saw a huge heart of light, and then vortexes of light again, that were this time dilating and contracting and spinning.... It was so magical, I was fascinated!

Later on, looking at the photos taken by myself and others who were there, to my delight I saw a purple ORB close to me. In that place of magnificent beauty, we are not alone.

Purple ORB – Sedona, AZ

At the Airport Energy Vortex, I felt energy in my palms and in my throat, and got a little bit dizzy. The rock formations were so impressive, they looked like petrified guardians protecting a secret treasure. That day I went back there at sunset and felt a huge amount of energy running through my body.

A few other tourists told me that they felt the same thing. The second day, I went down into a valley, where no other tourists were interested in going. I felt guided to sit down for a while in three different places. The energy was overwhelming. I drew the Reiki Symbols on stones, and gave Reiki to a few twisted trees that were like guardians there.

Then I walked on a narrow pathway till I got to the rock formation that looked like a group of people watching the whole place. Touching the stones, it felt really weird... the stones were cold but my palms became hot almost instantly, and a stream of energy went through my shoulders, as if someone gave me a hug. My physical eyes saw rocks, but my third eye saw movement, life... it felt like the rock formations were living beings to me. Turning around, I looked far away, as they would look, and realized that from there one could see the incredible symmetry, arrangement and positioning of Sedona's rock formations. Gazing at the most far away rock formation, soon the auras of each rock formation were revealed to me. The valley also was all filled with white light, like fog, but it wasn't fog... was that what is called an energy vortex?

More and more, my thoughts almost disappeared. The peace was so profound and the energy level so high!

At night, in my hotel room, all my body was flooded by currents of energy again: my palms, my feet, my crown chakra, my face, even my breasts, like never before. The vibration, the air, everything was a first time experience for me—it felt like I was between two worlds, at the boundary with another dimension. I was almost afraid to allow more miracles to unfold.

But hey! All that I'd seen and felt was a huge step in my level of allowance. The surroundings were a wonderful mirror for the soul. Sedona is, no doubt, a divine place. By observing the divine around, we are invited to observe the divine within.

Peace of mind! Simplicity! True love! It's all within our hearts. What we're looking for outside of us, it's actually already part of us...it's who we really are.

*

During my last day there, I went to the Chapel.

My crown was wide open the entire time. After lighting seven candles, I sat down in front of a huge Holy Cross and put my forehead on it. I prayed for Jesus from the bottom of my heart.

Then, I prayed to God to help me listen to Him.

After a while, looking at Jesus's statue, I asked: "Jesus, how come you, the most powerful healer of all times, were still crucified and still died on the cross?" The answer came almost instantly, deep in my heart:

The only security on Earth is in Spirit

It was exactly what I needed to hear at the moment. Many times I thought that by becoming a healer, God will protect me, will keep me away from diseases, will do me the "favor" of not getting contaminated with any contagious disease, or not becoming a victim of car accidents or any other kind of accident, simply because He won't want to waste someone whom He can work through.

Jesus in the Chapel – Sedona, AZ

I also remembered how, many years back, I wanted to be a healer for reasons that were not based on love, but rather on fear and desire for power: to be able to protect myself from people with bad intentions, by seeing their auras and controlling their minds; to build shields around myself, and then provoke my enemies in fights they would lose, simply by not being able to harm me through the shield in any way. I actually spent a huge amount of time imagining this kind of scenario, very similar to the scene in the movie *Matrix*, where Neal stops the bullets with the power of his mind. In front of Jesus's statue, there in Sedona, I remembered all those non-spiritual motivations for becoming a healer, and gave them up forever. They were all a big ego game.

Spiritual gifts are given to us for the purpose of serving humanity. Being humble is a hard lesson to learn, yet mandatory. Being humble includes accepting one's human condition, the fact of being incarnated. The human body is always vulnerable and needs to be protected, not exposed. I had to be reminded once more that the Spiritual gifts are not given to be abused, but used as God wishes.

As we give up our arrogance, we make room for the divine will to manifest through us.

If I had been given this answer by Divinity when I was young, it would have been so disappointing, but now I felt liberated, peaceful and light (light like a feather and also surrounded by shiny light). It is who I am, not what I can do, that makes me feel safe.

Knowing that my heart is filled with love makes me feel safe. My soul is given to the Divine.

After all that, I drew with water the Reiki symbols and the Holy Cross on my forehead, and left the Chapel with my heart filled with love and profound peace.

*

On my way out of Sedona, I stopped at Bell Rock one more time. In many places, there were spirals naturally carved in the hardest rocks. Were they really created by the Energy Vortex? Amazing!
One of the tourists said that in the Energy Vortex area, even trees are twisted, and indeed, right next to the mentioned hard rocks was a tree that had not only its trunk and branches twisted, but even the grass around was forming a spiral.

Twisted tree – Sedona, AZ

The tree was dead. I sat down, drew the Reiki symbols on my palms and placed them on its branches. With my eyes closed, I saw two vortexes of light next to each other that blended and transformed in a heart of light, and then, in a bigger vortex. What a wonderful vision! I didn't try to give it any meaning, but felt a deep connection with everything around, and felt *one* with the tree. Nature had its own pulse. It felt like even the dead tree had a heart.

So, I asked the tree:

"How come you, who grew up in the middle of an Energy Vortex, have died? If I lived here, I think I would be the most powerful."

The answer came, deep in my consciousness:

"Yes, but I had no water."

This answer, given by my higher self, brought to my attention that I should not neglect any area of my life. Being on a spiritual marathon, many times I put aside my social life, and especially my romantic life. It was time to bring balance to my earthly existence as a spiritual being.

Taking care of our bodies (shelter, food, exercise, safety, and wellness), our minds, our emotions and our spiritual lessons/missions is equally important for all of us.

All elements of life are equally important. All pieces of a whole are equally important. And we all are equally important, as rays of the same Divine Light.

*

Driving back to Phoenix, I was listening to a Native American CD, with drums and ceremonial songs, a trance-like music that was the best fit for the place and time in which I was. The road was straight, and nothing was there but huge cactuses on the side of the road. Far ahead, the sun was going down behind huge, beautiful mountains.... It was gorgeous! The peace and harmony and energy that I felt were indescribable. In fact just writing down my experience brings back the same intense feelings of joy and peace, and I love it!

I almost didn't talk with anyone during those three days. Even though normally I love to share any enthusiasm and positive experience with my friends, I didn't call them. It was an inward journey. I was like a peaceful lake, and that was a miracle. I've learned to recognize the miracles in little, simple things and felt so blessed, guided and protected in a natural and permanent way.

*

On the Thanksgiving night, I was alone in the airport for 14 hours, and I saw many people kissing and hugging each other in the waiting room, ready to celebrate together. I didn't complain nor pity myself for being alone, as I would have done before, not even for a second. Instead, I was thanking God for the blessing of being Thankful, and one of the ways I was waiting for my flight back to DC was to write down an updated list of things that I was grateful for.

The second part of Kasat's book also helped me appreciate the discomfort of the night spent on uncomfortable chairs of the airport, which was nothing compared with his discomfort traveling through Africa on public transportation.

Next morning, a few hours before my plane took off, I met Patrice, a wonderful seven-year-old girl. I smiled at the little girl and she smiled back at me, right before I was falling asleep in my chair one more time…. When I woke up, half an hour later, she was still there with her grandmother, crying. She was upset because they were asked to wait for three more hours and take the next available flight.

"Come here, sweetie. Why are you crying?" I asked. She told me why. "What time did you get here?" I asked. "7 AM" she responded, wiping her tears.
Holding her hand with love, I told her: "You see, I got here last night at 7 PM, and I'm not crying. Do you know how I spent my night?" I told her the whole story. Her face was now shiny. She smiled at me and said: "I wish you were my teacher." Her happiness made my heart sing. She saw something for herself, a new possibility for freedom of expression, friendship, and joy.

*

Along the length of this trip, I equally enjoyed being guided, as well as being of guidance. The opportunity to provide a little bit of inspiration to Patrice had awoken my desire to become a teacher. Not a school teacher, but a spiritual teacher.

My goals and vision about life evolved constantly as I was more and more tuned into the light and love of the Universe. After my trip to Sedona, I took the time and wrote down my new vision about how to serve humanity. Surprisingly, so many new ideas and goals never came to me before. They were in harmony with my new vibration.

For a few weeks, my vibration was very high, my mind was peaceful and my heart filled with joy. *Everything is a mirror*.... Even a brick... yes, a brick, can be a mirror. I realized that when, a week after my return from Sedona, I went to a yoga studio and, looking at a wall of bricks that was "ugly" before, now I saw it all shiny and beautiful!!!!! It was a mirror of my heart that was filled with love and light....

So funny, I had wanted to visit Sedona for many years, and when I returned and called my friend Geny from Romania and told her about my trip, she said: "Did you know that one of the most powerful places on Earth is in Carpati (the mountains in Romania)?" That reminded me of the personage in the book *The Alchemist*, who went on a long journey looking for a treasure that was actually buried in his own yard.... The real treasure, however, is the journey itself.

***

Learning more through dreams, life experiences, and Reiki practice

A few weeks after my return from Sedona, my vibration started to drop and it felt like I was stuck between two stages of life. Boredom, lack of motivation, lack of vivid dreams or even opportunities to practice Reiki as much as before—that was my new experience. It was clear to me that the only way to be happy in life is to enjoy the journey, whatever the destination is. Otherwise happiness lasts a second and then nothing is satisfying again.

To help myself through those moments, I just told myself that "this too shall pass."

Soon, I had a dream with many, many flowers that needed water. Wherever I went in my dream, I saw nothing but flowers.... The next day, I went to the massage school and had the opportunity to give five Reiki sessions in one day. The flowers in my dream were the people, and the water was the Reiki power, the "Life Giving Water." Giving the Reiki sessions, the feeling of fulfillment came back. "Ask and it is given"—I told myself. My break wasn't too long, just enough to really take in my fast transforming experiences from Sedona.

***

While practicing, I noticed how useful it is to learn the chakra descriptions (listed under the *Reiki Student's Handout* subchapter at the end of this book). Later, I used my observations in my teachings.

*

Here is a story related to serious imbalances in the root chakra—our life force energy center: a friend who suffered from serious colon problems asked me for a Reiki session. Scanning and letting the Reiki energy flow through my hands, I didn't feel much imbalance till my hands came in contact with his root chakra. Once there, all of a sudden I felt like the energy was vacuumed from my hands, and my hands started to hurt.

Remembering the description of the root chakra, I asked him if he grew up in fear. He was surprised to hear my question, and told me that yes, indeed, his father used to come home drunk at night threatening him and his mother. His sense of safety and security were altered to the point where his root chakra went seriously out of balance. As a result, now he was suffering from colon issues (see the root chakra chart provided in the Reiki handouts).

*

One night my friend Mari who was pregnant came over. We meditated together for a while, and my palms became really hot. I was visualizing Divine Light coming down through my crown as I was breathing in, then coming out through my palms into hers. The Divine Light was filling her, and she was smiling, she was blissful, she was so beautiful! I visualized Angels around her, and Jesus touching her head. Then, I heard the crystalline laughter of her unborn baby, who was swimming in fluid Divine Light. I thought that the amniotic liquid must be a perfect conductor of healing energy. Touching her belly, the baby started to move.

We both felt a great deal of energy, and prayed for her and the baby to be protected and blessed. I felt humbled and deeply honored to serve that way. The Angelic presence was unique.

About a month later, while in labor, she was courageous, confident and very strong. I admired her a lot. To support her and the baby, I wrote her name on a piece of paper and kept it in my hand for the entire length of time she was giving birth, visualizing them in a globe of light. While praying, the peace was so profound, and the presence of divine protection was very distinct. At 3:35 PM, all of a sudden my palms stopped burning, and I felt relief. About 20 minutes later I got a message from her husband, announcing that they're OK, and that their beautiful baby girl was born at 3:35 PM. Her name is Codruta, and later on, she became my first Goddaughter.

*

During a Reiki session, a friend had visions and saw beautiful colors. I was fascinated listening to her. We both felt relaxed, grounded, connected with the whole Universe.

*

A dear friend came over, and giving her a massage and Reiki session, she fell asleep. Her smile told me that she felt like a pampered child, safe, home! What a wonderful feeling, what a blessing, to share mutual pure joy and divine love, and totally relax! We are living in a world where we're running and working, and planning, and exhausting ourselves constantly.
I asked myself, "What if we would all love each other so genuinely? How would this world be?" Blissful! Divine! That's how it would be.

*

While visiting one of my cousins, she got a sharp tooth pain. After five minutes of Reiki, it stopped. It was a great surprise for both of us. A question came to my mind: "How much does our love for the people we're touching counts, when it comes to healing?" Looking back, I realized that our deep connection really generated more power; while holding my hands on her face, I said, "God, please love this beloved child of yours."

The heart chakra and palm chakras are connected. This is why our touch can heal through love!

*

At some point I did a series of Reiki sessions on my cousin's husband. He had a knee issue. In the beginning, pain was going up my hand, picking up the blockage and negative energy; this happens if there is resistance, blockage, and it feels like the energy doesn't get in. Pain or anxiety can be picked up from the receiver. In this stage of the session, I kept praying and sending light, and from time to time, shaking my hands toward the ground, with the intent to throw all negativity into a bowl filled with Divine Light.

After about 15 minutes, there was a shift; the blockage was being released, and the energy started to flow. It felt like a vacuum, sucking energy from my palm. At some point I visualized many hands of light—the Reiki Guide's hands—on top of my hands. With one hand on his hip and one on his knee, at some point I visualized his bone made of light, connecting at the middle of the distance. To me that image meant that now all cells of his leg are communicating through Divine Light. I moved my hands—one on his knee and one on his ankle. After about ten minutes the same visualization came to my mind—his bone made of light. Later, I realized that this kind of vision, even though very unclear, is teaching me, from case to case, about what it is or what to do. I told him to write down the following affirmation and read it every day: "I trust my body and I trust its wisdom."

After another fifteen to twenty minutes, he was filled with energy like a charged battery. A Reiki Guide came to my mind, pouring Divine Light on the top of my head from a big bucket.

Then, a nurturing kind of energy was flowing, and there was peace and light… and so it is every time at the end of a Reiki session.

The more I practiced Reiki, and the longer the session, the more my third eye opened.

***

My new vision about Romantic Love

The balance between my spiritual and earthly life needed attention. While taking the Reiki classes, my focus was my spiritual journey—no distractions, no fun, no emotional engagements. Getting to a point of completion, taking a deep breath, the teaching from Sedona came to my mind: "All elements of life are equally important."

What I most wanted was to be in love again.

An open heart is a way of living life, is being connected with the source. Sometimes we think that we protect ourselves by being less open for love but we actually disconnect ourselves from source. "Love is 24 hours sunshine" my friend Ra says.

An open heart could bring some tears but is being alive!

Even though I was single and living alone, I was never lonely. A spiritual journey is about our relationship with God. It is essential to be patient with ourselves and our loved ones. Earthquakes are shaking the whole life of the seeker as part of this growing process. Unless we're happy in our heart, nobody else will really make us happy. At that point, I was finally happy in my heart.

"Why not be in a relationship? I have a lot to give, and I love being in love… *love* is the air I'm breathing, and the light of healing. I feel love in my heart, with or without a man in my life, but I'm a human being too, not just a spirit, so I want to enjoy all earthly blessings as well. I want a relationship."

"Want is positive; need is not—is focusing on the lack of what you want" -- by Esther and Jerry Hicks (the Teachings of Abraham)

*

Despite my desire of being in a relationship, I still identified barriers, observing myself in the middle of important lessons to learn. Since my journey had been so fast for a while, and my vibration so much higher than before, my values were different, new. Therefore I had to take the time and write down what I now wanted in a relationship.

It took me weeks of focused intention, to first bring all the pieces of the puzzle together, and ask the Universe for the relationship I wanted.

My soul knew that I could only be in a relationship that helped do more, not less, spiritual work. Serving God first, avoids infatuation, selfishness and attachments. Love is true, only when we honor God's will for us. "You can't give what you don't have," so many spiritual teachers say. "How could I honor a human being if I don't honor my soul mission, if I don't honor God?"

Then, it clicked in my mind: "Serving God together means having a higher common purpose. Such a thing wants to be unfolded, for the highest good of all. Therefore, the whole Universe will make it happen. I do not have to worry about where to find him, nor has he to worry about where to find me. I only have to ask the Universe for what I want, be patient, recognize my future partner and trust God in my actions."

*

Here is how the Reiki teachings helped me define my new view about romantic love:

The harmony of all that is, is based on the same principles. Deepak Chopra gives an amazing example in this regard, in his book, *The Book of Secrets*. He gives humanity an idealistic model of living life, based on the rules governing the cells of our bodies. From microcosm to macrocosm, everything follows the same laws.

So, I thought about the analogy between our seven major chakras being balanced, as taught in the Reiki handouts, and a romantic relationship. I have discovered seven key elements that would create an ideal relationship:

Trust: When the root chakra is balanced, the person feels safe and secure. Only then can one trust oneself and others. When both partners have this chakra balanced, they can trust themselves and they can trust each other.

Passion: When the sacral chakra is balanced, one is able to be passionate, present, sensitive and considerate in intimacy.

Commitment and joy: When the solar plexus chakra is balanced, one has a strong will power, and therefore is able to honor commitments. Joy is also present and powerfully making life beautiful. Any true commitment is made with joy, and kept with the support of one's will power.

True love: When the heart chakra is balanced, one can love oneself, and only then can truly love others. Before we love ourselves, we might think we love others, but in fact we need them, more than we love them. Attachments are a direct result, as well as selfish behavior.

Communication: When the throat chakra is balanced, one expresses oneself at one's best. The way they talk, the way they listen. The quality of love is in direct proportion with the quality of communication.

Intuition: When the third eye chakra is balanced, one is intuitive, has the vision of life, of one's mission, of their relationship together, knows beyond words and feels the deepest corners of the other's soul.

A higher common purpose: When the crown chakra is balanced, one has attained a solid connection with God. The couple can have a higher purpose—they see above themselves. Their desires are aligned with divine will. They serve humanity more and more. They are driven by their purpose. They are blessed, blissful, and infinitely loved by God.

Note: This new vision about spiritual romantic love is further developed in another book, entitled *Seven Chakras Love*.

*

Any relationship will always be subject to development and growth, as we all are on an infinite spiritual journey. This is why it was important for me to look in a potential partner for the possibility and commitment toward such a goal, not for perfection.

The whole Universe wanted my vision to come true, but in divine time. It took me a while to understand what that meant. While still waiting to meet my partner, I was told by my teachers that it wasn't the right time for me to be in a relationship of any kind, before I built at least the foundation, and the walls of my "house"—my spiritual mission.

Placing an order to God is not enough. We have to learn how to wait and allow the unfolding of the blessings we are asking for. Praying for something to come true is like planting seeds. Digging every day to see if they're growing doesn't help. Planting too many doesn't help either.

A long time went by till I really shared the mutual romantic love of my dreams, but the seeds were planted deep in my heart right in those moments of pure co-creation with the divine.

"Love is the ability and willingness to allow those that you care for to be what they choose for themselves without any insistence that they satisfy you." – Wayne Dyer

***

Reiki and Christianity

For a long time, while being on an intensive spiritual development pathway, I didn't feel okay other than talking, thinking, and acting from the light of my soul. I was afraid that I might get lost otherwise in chaos, depression, bad influences, addictions, etc.... I didn't even watch TV, go to a club nor have a glass of wine. That made me lose contact with the world around me more and more. After a while, though, it became clear to me that I can't possibly lose my soul mission, and as a result, I became more open and felt safe in any environment, allowing myself to be human, and be of service for others when needed.

I used to judge other spiritually developed people for things that I thought should not be part of their equation anymore. Then, I understood more and more that expectations are Ego's weapons in action killing relationships and the oneness with humans and with the Divine. Everyone has their own right time for everything. "Just share your heart," my inner voice said.

Feeling strong enough in my transformation, I started to spend more time talking with strangers on public transportation, in parks and coffee shops. Many people were happy to hear new concepts about healing and spirituality; however, a man was very offended by my "healer mindset," and asked me: "What religion are you? Isn't Reiki against your religion?" It made me think. I knew it's not, not at all, but didn't know how to explain and give someone like him the necessary knowledge to freely choose what to believe.

His attitude was simply based on what he'd been taught in the past, and there was a gap. Challenges are always opportunities. Even though he irritated me, I knew that was an opportunity to focus on my self-expression, and deeply look inside, and ask for guidance.

"Everything that irritates us about others can lead us to an understanding of ourselves." - Carl Jung

I knew that by asking for guidance, my words will come out for the highest good of my audience. My willingness to share what I've been taught grew even more.

So I sat down and wrote, from the bottom of my heart, my view about Reiki and Christianity:

Considering the Miracles that Jesus Christ performed, we all can agree that He was the most powerful healer on Earth despite one's religious beliefs. Jesus Christ is Divine Love! In His teachings, Jesus doesn't ask us to be healers, nor does he prohibit us from being healers. He just teaches us to learn how to truly love! Isn't it interesting to know that the heart chakra is connected with the palm chakras, and the healing powers are growing in direct proportion with our capacity of love? As we follow Jesus's teachings and open our hearts, we all will eventually become healers. It is less important what the healing technique is called. Healing comes from God, it happens only with God's will, and it is divine love! The practitioner is simply a tool in God's hand, a channel.

Who can be a tool in God's hands? Anyone! Jesus picked his disciples from the crowd.

They were simple people, but they had pure hearts. They were taught, they were initiated, and they have performed many miracles throughout their lives. "Am I chosen?" one may ask; the answer is in our hearts. If you dare to dream, you are called to be a healer; if you're a healer without even asking, you've asked before you were born. It's not an accident, it is meant to be.

Jesus said "Follow Me." What He really meant was "Love! *Be love!*" As Sonia Choquette says in her book, *Diary of a Psychic*, "*The ultimate lesson on Earth is Unconditional Love.*"

Becoming creatures of Unconditional Love, we experience the Heaven in our hearts, in the Now!

***

Steps Forward in Psychic Development

Opportunities to practice Reiki were constantly there for me, and that taught me a lot and gave me great joy and fulfillment. However, after a while I felt that becoming a Reiki Master was just a small step on an infinite spiritual journey. Now what? I needed spiritual guidance, and an impulse to move on. So I went back to Bob—my psychic reader and spiritual teacher.

He told me that I was between two stages on my journey, and I should allow myself two weeks of rest, and reconnect with my Romanian spiritual joy. He also told me that I was about to have a very challenging upcoming year, learning something every day, teaching a lot, taking on my students' lives, increasing my strength of spirit. He taught me to keep a journal of my students' and clients' journeys, and never refuse a student, even though I might not like some of them or not have time for them. "They're all sent by God."

He confirmed an old thought that I had in mind, and said that indeed I met Jesus in person, and I was fascinated by his healing. Later on that night I looked again at the photo I have at home, with the Samaritan woman and Jesus, and felt Jesus's teachings flowing through my veins: "If you drink this water you'll be thirsty again, but if you drink the water I'm offering you, not only will you never be thirsty again, but you'll transform into a flowing fountain of life giving water."

Bob confirmed that Reiki helps develop psychic abilities. He said that I used to have all spiritual gifts in past lives, and I was a healer many times.

In this life, for so long I felt it was unfair not to have these gifts. Finally I realized that, because I chose to be a teacher, it helps me more if I have to go through the process myself, in order to be able to help others find their gifts within. That fits perfectly who I am—a being who's only really learning, expanding awareness, growing and teaching by being in the game.

At the end, he concluded: "Spirits know you're ready."

His words and his energy shifted something in me. I felt great.

*

So, during the following two weeks, I called my friend Geny in Romania, and my cousins who are very connected with the spiritual realm, read again the book translated from English to Romanian by my first esoteric teacher, Alexandru E. Russu, and prayed a lot for my grandmother Roza, my first source of divine love. It was indeed great advice to follow and it rejuvenated me a lot.

My meditation time was more peaceful—the mind rested better and the soul charged more.

One morning I dreamed that I was in my room, jumping from one wall to another, walking on the ceiling, but thinking that I could fall. I jumped across the room and grabbed my wooden Holy Cross from the shelf, praying, saying Our Father a few times in a row, till I woke up.

It was a lesson about the feeling of being safe during an out of body experience, in direct proportion with the power of my faith.

It made me happy once more to see that my faith is deep and the prayer comes to serve me from the deepest corners of consciousness.

The following week, a beautiful dream reinforced my joy of being on the journey even more. It seemed that I was in a cavern, looking for a treasure. It was a representation of the self-search, the digging into the subconscious, hidden powers within. Then I was going up on stairs, and they were old, full of dust. I was finding a little silver or crystal screw in the dust on each and every step—a metaphor of the priceless lessons learned along the way. Then I arrived in a huge cavern, filled with colorful, shiny shells.

Exactly two weeks after seeing Bob, opportunities to practice Reiki appeared again. I felt focused, and my spiritual joy was back, renewed and powerful.

*

One of my favorite Spiritual Teachers today is Sonia Choquette. I've learned many things from her, and applied many of her teachings. One of the most inspiring and empowering things I've read in one of her books is this:

> *"Who I am is a spiritual being,*
> *Protected by angels,*
> *Healed by my healers,*
> *Taught by my teachers,*
> *Helped by my runners,*

*And
I am infinitely loved by God"
(Sonia Choquette)*

It doesn't happen to me very often, but once I got the flu.
Doing Reiki on myself and listening to one of Sonia's
books on CD helped me to keep going. The tendency was
to fall into depression, to remember all the things that I
didn't have but wanted in my life and all the people that I
was missing so much, but they were far away. Hearing
Sonia's empowering affirmation, instead of being in a
pity party and feeling alone while being sick, I chose to
be happy, surrounded by Angels.

*By believing in God, we believe in possibilities, in what
we didn't already know, in solutions, opportunities and
new ways. Expecting and allowing, we're powerful
beyond measure, in the now.*

*

Sometimes I had glimpses of magic—moments when I
saw so clearly the possibility of being an instrument for
miracles. "The Divine Light makes miracles through me;
my spirit can fly and help others who are far away; I can
transcend through meditation and Reiki distant healing, I
can coordinate my body and be wide awake and
focused." Wow... "I should spend more time dreaming,
imagining: flying, swimming like a fish, running like the
wind, traveling through galaxies, seeing the Earth like a
cherry in my hand." Dreamlike awareness—the power of
joyful imagination—has been recommended by so many
spiritual teachers throughout time.

"Imagination is the true magic carpet." — Norman Vincent Peale, a minister and author of inspirational books

To fulfill my intention of spending more time dreaming and creating my psychic pathway, I took Sonia Choquette's online class, *Psychic University*, which was absolutely amazing! As part of the online class, I practiced dreamlike awareness, and invented a psychic persona:

"My name is Magic Oneness, and I'm a feminine version of Merlin. Magic actually means *oneness* with God and all creation. Oneness is the way for magic to manifest. I'm telepathically communicating with all healers. I am fully psychic and a very powerful healer. I can have out of body experiences at will and be on a spiritual mission, finding lost people, healing others during astral traveling, while asleep. I am light like a feather dancing in the wind. I have a spiritual partner, and together, and along with many others, we are raising the Earth's vibration. We serve the 'New King of Humans' in his effort of manifesting peace through oneness on our planet."

Inventing a psychic persona had a huge positive impact on me. It basically triggered the possibility of transformation, of miraculous instant manifestation of any desires that are aligned with my soul mission. The feeling was powerful, it gave me wings. Try for yourself, and you will see.

To my surprise, about six month later, Bob told me that Saint Germain works through me, heals through me, helps me write this book, and will help me in a few years in a bigger project. One of Saint Germain's incarnations was Merlin.

Another very important part of this online course by Sonia Choquette was to think about what our barriers are, in the way of being psychic. I've discovered that at times I was still attached to things or people that I wanted too much in my life, refusing to see the reality. This is called delusion. This is a major obstacle in the way of a psychic—*as long as someone doesn't accept reality, she/he will always argue with the voice of intuition, will edit intuitive messages, and finally, reject being psychic.* I accepted myself for who I was but then chose to learn to accept reality, with peace and ease, right away. Making a conscious effort in removing attachments, later I participated in Shamanic Sacred Ceremonies that are specifically designed to do so. As a result, more clarity, more powerful intuitive vibes, and more powerful communication with the spirit world unfolded in my life.

***

Shaman Manin – my "Shamama"

Hearing about the opening of a metaphysical shop in the Washington DC area, I felt called to go. To my surprise, one of the main organizers was an amazing woman whom I had met a few months before. My calling was powerful. I didn't know why till I got in, but once there, I recognized who was calling me in an instant: Shaman Manin. The first impulse when seeing her was: "I want to learn from her." We introduced ourselves to each other and briefly talked. We exchanged contact information, and soon I left and didn't hear about her for almost three months; but we finally connected and ever since she has been my beloved Spiritual Teacher. Since she is a Shaman, and she is protective and loving as a mother to me, I'm sometimes calling her "Shamama."

While taking an "Energetic Expansion Attunements" class with her, I felt lots of energy flowing through my body. I came back home and lay down observing it for hours…. She told me to do the attunements twice a day. By doing so, I felt energy flowing through different areas of my body all the time. I felt more peace and clarity right away. These attunements are gifts from the higher powers, from beings of light who are channeling through her for the highest good of humankind. She calls these light beings "Councils."

It took me a while to grasp and understand what Councils means, but little by little, Councils started to work through me too. A listing of Councils working through Shaman Manin can be found below, as she had shared with me in response to my many questions.

"When I refer to 'Councils,' (notice it's plural) I am including those beings from the Inter-Galactic Federation of Light, the Healing Councils, as well as the Ascended Masters, Prophets, deities, and beings from many dimensions, galaxies, and planets. I work with the following Council members daily and I begin my energy sequences with:

I am SoDalited to invite my Councils who are here for my highest good and the highest good of humankind, PachaMama, the plants, animals and waters.
Sirius, Pleaides, Sananda, Alpha Centauri, Draco, Sagittarius, Arcturus, Lemuria,
Anilam, Mizar, Kochab, Orion, Betelgeuse, Rigel.
Amin-Ra, Horus, Isis, Osiris, Maat, Thoth,
Merlin, Mercury/Hermes, Apollo/Zeus, Neptune
Apus, Ascended Masters & Prophets (Jesus Christ, Buddha, Muhammad), Ancients & Ancestors
Arch Angels Michael, Gabriel, Sandalphon, Raphael, the Elohim,
DK, Yamantaka, Quan Yin, Tara
Mother Mary, the Virgin(s), Mary Magdalene
All my crystals. Manin's personal angel, the Fairy Godmother, Charles Dickens, the Toolmaster, the Energy master, power animals and others who are here for the highest good.

"Then for the client, I might call in certain Shamanic brothers/sisters on the planet, depending on the healing, and I invite their Council members & ancestors.

"Whoever needs to work with us steps forward and guides us, directs the appropriate frequency that the person needs. Manin serves as the channel. When I am working with a person, I simply focus on the incoming light energies or pictures. If I am directed to a certain place in a person's body, I will increase/decrease the energy to that area, as guided. If I see or hear something the person needs to know, I tell them. Manin doesn't want to know all the nitty-gritty details of how things happened to get to this moment in time. If someone wants me to look into the history, okay, but I try not to be invasive."

***

"I am so blessed to be your student!" I told her. In this life, I started being Manin's student between my first Reiki I teachings and my first Reiki II teachings. The stories following in this chapter transcend through a much longer period of time, and sure enough, I will continue to be Manin's student for many years.

Once I asked her if it's okay for me to share the attunements with my friends. Her answer confirmed my feelings of infinite bliss unfolding every time I've been sharing spiritual gifts: "When you share these attunements with people, you are friends on the soul level. One could never purchase that abundance.

It is earned through respect of self, Spirit and all that is," Manin said.

Recognizing the feeling of knowing her for ever, I asked her directly if she knows whether or not we met in previous lives.

"You have been my student in past lives. You already know these teachings. We create Oneness through Spirit, people, animals, Mother Earth and the Universe. We are Ambassadors of Peace. Our job is to spread love and happiness and help people raise their vibrations. One ought to be ready to seize all opportunities to share love and peace."

I really thought about it. So many things crossed my mind! So many pieces of a big puzzle came together.... "Yes, I love all people, have friends from all over the world, respect all religions, stand for harmony and peace between people, love animals and nature, can only think about Peace as being *the way*, and love is the air I'm breathing, the blood flowing through my veins.... Wow! It is really not by chance that I felt this way more and more..." "Ambassadors of Peace... Ambassadors of Peace..." yes, that's exactly what I've been my whole life, without even thinking about it.

What a blessing, what a soul reunion! It made even more sense for me that I've gotten to come to the United States, and why I settled in Washington DC. I started to practice the Energetic Expansion Attunements every day and incorporated them in my healing sessions.

Shaman Manin said that these attunements can be incorporated in my Reiki practice and will increase the power of it. She is a Reiki Master herself and uses them all the time. "Thank you so much, Manin, for teaching me with so much love and joy!"

Shaman Manin gave me energetically enhanced photos that will help me and anyone who sees them to enhance their vibration of each energetic level (Cosmic, Monadic, Athmic, Buddhic, Mental, Emotional and Etheric Body; then, crown, third eye, throat, heart, solar plexus, sacral and root; then, molecular).

"Focus as long as possible on highly vibrational things," Manin said.

In the beginning I felt overwhelmed with my new homework, wondering when in the world was I going to do all this. But then it occurred to me that I was still spending time thinking useless thoughts, which can be replaced with powerful thoughts such as running these energies. That's very important – *to keep ourselves busy with what really supports us on our spiritual journey, to feed the Light Within, and create new patterns of thought and emotion.* We are creatures of habit, and little by little I understood that *being happy and joyful is a habit* just like it is to be sad, worried or depressed. It takes work, it takes time, but it's worth doing it. My life blossomed more and more as my old patterns were replaced with new ones that better served my spirit and everyone else around.

I am connected with divine powers for my highest good and the highest good of all concerned.

———

83

From top to bottom, I have been attuning myself daily, and felt an inward harmony like never before. To help myself in the process, I printed the photos and placed them on my door in a particular order, and spent time daily looking at them, practicing empowering affirmations and meditating.

The sequence is a comprehensive set covering all energy centers, and it is provided for you, along with the related empowering affirmations, in my book, *Focused on Spirit*, under the chapter "Your daily Energetic Expansion Attunements - channeled by Shaman Manin."

Attunements from top to bottom: SoDalited, Eholim, Reiki symbols, Healing-Cleansing Thought Form, Santara-Cusgal, Quan Yin Cubed, Flood Light.

For a detailed description of most Energetic Expansion Attunements, please visit Shaman Manin's website: http://**veinsofsilver**.org

***

Below are ways in which I've been using the Energetic Expansion Attunements for the highest good.

One morning, when I started to meditate, my grandmother Roza's spirit came and encouraged me to send my mom The Flood Light Program (highly effective in case of suicidal situations or accidents).

At that point I had been running the Energetic Expansion Attunements every day for about a month, but never thought about sending them to anyone yet. I didn't wonder why my grandmother Roza wanted me to do that and just obeyed her wish. The true connection with my grandmother Roza's spirit had been established about a year before that time, when I finally really accepted her death. The joy of having her in my life as a spirit guide transformed the access to her from untouchable to real. That morning really unfolded this real and effective connection. A few hours after running Flood Light on my mom, I opened my e-mail and found a message sent by her the day before. She was describing what she was going through lately, saying: "Yesterday I just couldn't take it anymore and wanted to throw myself in the river." Wow…my grandmother Roza (her mom) really gave me good advice from the spirit world….

Calling my mom, I found that she was now feeling much better. She was happy to hear that she received Flood Light's beautiful energy.

*

About a month later, all my family had serious health issues at the same time. "How can I help all of them?" I asked. The answer didn't seem to come from myself but rather from a higher power—the Councils: "Group distant healing session."

The description below is not a teaching; it is simply an example of how guidance and imagination work together:

1. Prayed, drew all Reiki symbols on my palms and on each of their photos
2. Placed my hands over their heads, connecting (mom, dad and my grandmother Mama Nana who was very old and sick in bed for over three years at the time)
3. Imagined that we were all meditating together for a few minutes holding hands
4. Imagined them encapsulated in a globe of light; drew all Reiki symbols, Flood Light and Quan Yin Cubed attunements on the globe. The symbols entered in the fluid light and healed them—they were all like happy babies in uterus.
5. At some point, visualized an Angel pouring light on the globe…. And as that light entered they all started to laugh and be filled with health, joy and happiness….
6. At the end of the session my grandmother Roza's spirit came through and gave me a hug.

*

Sharing these new experiences with Shaman Manin, I was still in a place of wonder about the power and the truthfulness of my healing sessions and my visions. She said:

"Your intent is everything!"

Our thoughts have power. "Thoughts are things," Prentice Mulford and many other spiritual teachers said. We are not alone in this. Doubts would only attract doubt—and the magic would be detoured from its powerful flow.

A good and powerful intent attracts good and powerful guidance.

Feel free to create! Our spirit creates. Nothing has to be done in a particular way. That would close the door between our spirit and the Universal Consciousness. Trust your light within!

***

Once I found myself visualizing a spiral of light during a group meditation. The spiral was going up like a cone, and then it opened again. Next, I visualized the center of our galaxy, and from there was poured light in the middle of us, and we were surrounded by the steam—like the vapors of a huge waterfall—a waterfall of life-giving water... the feeling of grandeur shifted us to a higher state of consciousness. About two months later, during my first visit to Shaman Manin's house, I was shocked to see a drawing of that visualization in her house. She told me that the drawing was from Councils, channeled through her, and it represents a powerful Energetic Expansion Attunement. She had sent it to me two months before, but never told me.

*

Another time, Manin told me that I have a new spirit guide, who had her hands in a certain position. I meditated using that and asked, "What is your name?" and it came to my mind "Izabell." A few weeks later, my psychic reader and teacher, Bob, told me that I have a new Native American guide, and her name is Silverbell.

*

Shaman Manin gave a healing session to a young woman and allowed me to assist her. I was just scanning the girl's chakras with my Reiki pendulum. Her knee had a problem, and the pendulum was accurate. I said, "Past life," and felt guided to do so. Manin listened to Councils and said, "Your leg was cut from the knee to save your life, in the Civil War, in Gettysburg." The girl was astonished to hear that, got up and said, "Oh, my God, I can't stand that place! I'm avoiding it all the time and drive 100 miles away around it." Manin sent her healing energy, and then the pendulum moved almost perfectly. The small hesitation of its movement made me say, "You are now okay; you just have to learn how to walk again like a person with two legs."

*

Sleeping in Manin's room, surrounded by six shelves filled with attuned quartz crystals at work, is not a joke… it's as energizing as taking a class or receiving an initiation. In the morning, as I opened my eyes, I felt all my chakras moving, and especially my heart chakra was so filled with energy, it sent me outside to breathe, and to share, by sending distant healing to all people in my life.

*

She taught me a meditation that helps me let go of the controlling mechanism and surrender to the higher powers: "Imagine you are entering into the blue water of a beautiful lake. Diamonds are floating in the sun, on the surface. You go deeper and deeper and lie down on your back.

Jesus and your Reiki guides, spirit guides, your grandmother, your first teacher (Alexandru E. Russu) are sustaining you to float. You are safe. It's beautiful...you feel so good! You trust. You are blissful, filled with joy, love and peace. Then, you're coming back and your friends are welcoming you on the land."

*

We were making leather crafts together, talking about so many things, and about how to incorporate all the spiritual teachings in the daily life. Being a Shaman doesn't manifest a few hours a day, but 24 hours a day.

*

We've shared about our loving relationships with friends and family. Talking about my grandmother Roza, and the fact that she looked like a Native American, Manin asked Councils about her and told me: "Roza was a Native American Shaman in a past life, and he—a man in that life—was blind but very connected with the Great Spirit. He asked for gifts and received the gift of clairvoyance from the Great Spirit."

Not long after this conversation I found the following statement in the book *Indian Spirit*:
"I am blind and do not see the things of this world; but when the Light comes from Above, it enlightens my heart and I can see, for the Eye of my heart sees everything. The heart is a sanctuary at the center of which there is a little space, wherein the Great Spirit dwells, and this is the Eye by which He sees all things and through which we see Him.

If the heart is not pure, the Great Spirit cannot be seen. The man who is pure contains the Universe in the pocket of his heart." - Black Elk, Oglala Lakota

*

An indescribable feeling of being home nourished my soul. Manin is more than a teacher, she is soul-family, protecting energy, power through spiritual love. She teaches through love, I learn through love. That's the way to learn and teach, allowing the universal energy to flow freely.

To add the Reiki power to our spiritual connection, I reviewed the Reiki Master class with her and received from her a Reiki Attunement. That happened much later, when I already had been teaching all Reiki levels. She showed me how to incorporate a few Shamanic practices into my Reiki Sessions, which I appreciated very much, and so did my students.

I also took classes on *Healing with Crystals* with Shaman Manin. A whole new Universe opened up for me. It expanded my awareness about crystals as being real, alive, intelligent, powerful tools for healing and connective with the higher intelligence. It helped me understand why the Amethyst crystal that I had for a while takes any headaches away every time in less than ten minutes, and so much more.

Then I officially became a student of Multicultural Shamanism. There was so much to learn from Shaman Manin! Magical journey!

***

Even though my life blossomed more and more, once I was still down, and asked for help. Manin and Councils responded:

"There is much negativity and anger being released into the atmosphere these days. Do not let it affect you." – Manin
"Your soul is beautiful. It is filled with love. Joy is yours." – *Councils*
"First you must take care of yourself and run your energies so that you are in top form.

When you have a good foundation and are running at top speed, then you are not influenced by people or circumstances, and your own comfort zone expands. As a healer, you will find yourself working with people of all circumstances, from the lowest vibrations to the highest. To do this work effectively, you must maintain balance yourself."

"Do not allow yourself to be distracted by other people's chaos, because that's all it is (chaotic energies bouncing around in all directions without intent to direct the energy). It's not that people are 'bad'—it's that *many people simply don't know the energies of universal love, compassion, grace and forgiveness.* It is up to us, the teachers and healers to show them that there is a path of Joy and Happiness." – Manin

*

My life transformed and my spirituality blossomed more and more as I was following Manin's teachings. I am deeply honored and very grateful.

You may feel the calling of finding a teacher too. Your desire to learn and grow will lead you there. Your guides will lead you there. You have already made a pact with your teacher before you were born. Your teacher is waiting for you, when you are ready.

"Each person on this planet may walk the path of Joy and Happiness, if they so choose." – The Councils

***

Teaching Reiki – a Transformational Soul Mission

What really inspires people is not so much what teachers are saying, as it is who they are becoming. If by looking at a teacher people see happiness, they want it for themselves too. In that very moment, they are half transformed. Looking in my own eyes, I saw happiness, love, and a huge willingness to share my light within. Later, a prospective student confirmed that: during a Reiki workshop, I asked: "Why are you here today?" She answered: "Because I see that you are so happy, optimistic, full of light and energy, and I want to know what helped you get there."

Yes, I was happy, optimistic and full of light and energy, and willing to share my source.

Every one of us has unique ways of learning and practicing, and without this freedom the new practitioners would never find the most amazing and powerful experiences. Why? Because we are co-creators with God! Without the freedom to create, we are disconnected from source. That being said, I invite you to let this chapter be a source of inspiration.

"Words don't teach…. it is life experience that brings the knowing. Before you can teach you must know" – Esther and Jerry Hicks (the Teachings of Abraham)

What I've learned by teaching Reiki I

About six months after becoming a Reiki Master, I felt ready to initiate others (to pass Reiki attunements). I really wanted to start with a beloved person in my life, and the opportunity arrived right away—my cousin Tania, who, less than a year before, had received Reiki through my hands after her brain surgery. She was now ready to receive her first Reiki attunement.

We meditated together, felt each other's energy, and prayed. I visualized a light being between us, touching each of us with a wing of light, blessing our spiritual partnership, then placing his hands on top of our hands.

Then, I visualized many colorful stars around us, and a white light surrounding us. At that point *I wasn't able to tell whether or not that was imagination, or visualization. Later I learned that it's always in the middle—we are God's co-creators.* I was a little bit nervous, not fully trusting yet the unseen miracle of passing an attunement, and especially, not fully trusting myself. Even though I had done my homework in advance, I was still double-checking every step against my Reiki handouts.

Her cat was watching, very focused, the entire time. We were later wondering if cats are psychic.

We were grateful, humbled and peaceful afterwards. I felt a lot of heat going through me for the next couple of days. She didn't, but like never in the last twenty years, she slept every day at noon for two or three hours. Later on it occurred to me that her nervous system was actually recovering after the surgery.

The attunement served first of all as a powerful healing session for her.

We found ourselves connected to a higher level through Reiki. We both believed even more. I'll be grateful forever to her, for trusting me and letting me pass her the Reiki attunement. My confidence grew and something deep in my heart knew that I would give more attunements soon.

The following weekend, I spent hours in meditation, gratefulness, oneness, asking for spiritual gifts, defining my intent. While giving the Reiki attunement, I automatically received one too, and as a result, my vibration was higher. I felt free and self expressed, guided, protected and taught by a higher power.

Any time we are connected to the light and love within ourselves, we feel whole. Having a magic wand in our hands could challenge the ego. All of a sudden, we are ambassadors of miracles. Only pure love could dissolve this challenge. When we really care, we share our blessings with love, not with arrogance.

*

During the following month I passed another two Reiki attunements to someone who had been a Reiki II for many years, and wanted reinforcement before pursuing the third level.

*

On a Saturday morning, the first thing I felt was compassion and love for Maribeth, one of my massage classmates, whom I'd never felt that close to before. It surprised me, but I didn't give it any importance. Later that day though, she told me that she was sick and wanted a Reiki session. My first impulse was to do that, but then I had an insight: to actually pass her a Reiki attunement, which she planned on receiving through me in the near future anyway. She agreed, and received the attunement unexpectedly that day. We welcomed the Reiki partnership in our life with much joy. Then I remembered that Bob, my spiritual consultant, had told me that I would have premonitions about my students. So true! Thank you, Bob! A week later, Maribeth said that surgery was avoided because of her Reiki attunement. She was really happy for that, and so was I. Little by little, we became great spiritual partners and good friends.

"When you serve humanity, opportunities are never in short supply" - Anonymous

*

These isolated experiences as a Reiki Teacher gave me enough confidence to expand. I felt that it was really important to reorganize my knowledge, express my inspiration, and reach out to find Reiki students. I went through a marathon of sleepless nights and sacrificed weekends to put together my website (www.YourLightWithin.com) and revise the Reiki handouts provided by my first Reiki Teacher.

As soon as the website was up and running and my Reiki materials updated, things unfolded with ease. One day a friend told me about a website, www.meetup.com, where I might find a new Reiki network and potential students.

Happy to open a new door, browsing through the members of the website, I sent out a few messages to people interested to learn. I was committed to do my best with all people around me, without being disappointed by their choice.

Only one person responded to my e-mails. His name is Wanakhavi. He said, "I want to learn and I want to teach. Could you give me some spiritual guidance?"

We tried to correspond by e-mail but it would have taken too much time to write, so we started to have weekly meetings, with amazing spiritual conversations, meditation sessions, Reiki and homework.

It wasn't even two weeks after we met when he asked me to send him a distant Reiki session. He wanted to experience and see how it works. We decided on a late hour, before he went to sleep. Starting the session, I sensed that he was actually falling asleep. I visualized him in his bed, and his silver cord—the cord of light connecting the body with the spirit—going up. He was traveling in his sleep. My hands of light gave more light to his silver cord. The next thing I visualized was a huge dragon, on his left side, protecting him. My interpretation was that the dragon was a metaphor for his guardian Angel.

Then an African statue of a powerful spiritual guide came to mind, and soon, Wanakhavi's photo overlapping the statue. The knowing, the feeling associated with this was that Wanakhavi is a very powerful, ancient soul, who's now ready to wake up again to an abundant spiritual life, who is now ready to blossom. My higher self knew that my homework, my mission, is to support him in this process, as if there is a contract between our souls in this regard. The distant Reiki session ended there.

Imagination or visualization—I was still asking myself what the truth was. It was more of a knowing than anything else. I shared with him but didn't make that session be the leading force of our interactions of beliefs. It wasn't even two month later, though, when he reconnected with his spiritual gifts, found that he is an old spirit with a great spiritual mission on Earth, and that one of his spirit guides is being seen as a dragon. On his journey, he had a lot of challenges, very similar to the one I'd been through not long before.

That was telling a lot about why *certain people can most support each other—through their common learning experience.* Awareness only grows through real "face to face" experiences. It felt like I was guided what to tell him; however, it was necessary for him to experience every step. "I can't really protect you, just tell you how you can protect yourself when you need it," I said to him.

Wanakhavi taught and helped me at least as much as I taught and helped him. He invited me to go with him to a Sunday service at a Spiritualist Church. As soon as we got there, to my surprise, I saw Sue, an amazing woman whom I briefly met before. The church became a home for me. Soon I started to teach Reiki there, and later became one of the healing arts practitioners of the church.

In the beginning, a good friend and Reiki classmate taught with me. It was a great experience for both of us, to share our teaching experience. Our first class was actually a group of friends who were inspired by our spiritual journey and wanted to expand their tools for spiritual growth. Our friendship transformed into spiritual partnership, step by step; we all learned from each other, we all grew together more and more, and formed a very solid foundation for something bigger.

*

One day I met Carl, who was so eager to learn Reiki. He wanted me to teach him right away. I only had one unscheduled afternoon that week and felt overwhelmed. I almost said no, but then remembered Bob telling me, "Never say no, they are sent to you by God." So I took a deep breath and prayed... and the answer came: *If God wants me to serve Him, He'll give me the power to do so.* Two days later I met Carl at a coffee shop and went through half of the Reiki I materials. It was more than delightful. He is a blessing for the world, a true leader, and sure enough, "my joy spirit." Our class was rejuvenating my spirit, and the reward from God for accepting to serve beyond my comfort level was well appreciated.

*

Teaching is always different, as the students are different. I've been learning so many different things along the way, and by being open, my Reiki teaching evolved into something bigger.

After a while I changed the name of the Reiki I class into: "The Spiritual Power Switch – Reiki I incorporated." Reiki to me is a piece of a bigger picture in one's spiritual development.

I noticed that before passing Reiki attunements, my throat chakra opens up, and while I pray and meditate with the initiated person, I'm usually allowed to see their spirit guides. This is how I saw grandfathers, grandmothers, guardian Angels, spirit guides from all times, from all religious and ethnic backgrounds, Master guides, and once even a huge tree, representing the spirit of the forest.

Cho-Ku-Rei – The Reiki symbol for physical healing

While passing the Reiki attunement, once I had the vision of a Rastafarian old man, with long locks to his ankles, blowing smoke over the hair of the student. He was drawing the Reiki symbols with smoke over the student. At the end of the attunement, I shared with my student what I saw and he said, "I know him. He was my spiritual mentor. I lived in a cave with him for three months, in Ethiopia."

The "AHA" moment for me was then to acknowledge the unspoken, dismissed details that were in my vision: the old man got up from a chair carved in stone.

Once, the soul of my esoteric teacher came through. I found myself looking into the eyes of my student just the way he used to look into my eyes. Teachings came out of my mouth, in a light trance. My student's old pain shifted into bliss. She accepted all her past traumatic experiences with ease and saw herself in a new light: "I am chosen."

Later I learned that my student and I had a lot in common and that perhaps attracted my teacher's spirit, to guide her and protect her on her new journey.

Each of the new initiates has seen more and more changes as time went on—it's an inward transformation and growth, not a miracle. It could take some time to feel the change, but it is more intense if the new practitioner uses Reiki and meditates on a daily basis. For some of the very advanced ones, it could be an insignificant change from where they already are.

Some students are feeling tingling or heat from time to time in different areas; others are just sleeping more, or sleeping less and feeling full of life.
Some have more vivid dreams; some feel more safe and balanced; some have things changing in their lives; some don't feel much but yet there is a subtle change that creates a new vibration, a new context for their lives.

One student felt a new level of freedom; another one found his voice; another one cared more; another one noticed nature; another one found herself on a mission—she drew the Reiki symbol to bring in the energy for the homeless in the park. Examples are covering a wide variety of positive changes.

Sometimes amazing metaphors are being revealed in dreams: one Reiki student told me that he dreamed that all his flesh was falling, and then it was replaced with new flesh made of bright light. A female student dreamed that her reproductive system was healed, and soon after she became pregnant—a blessing expected for a while.

It is so different from one person to the next that I can't really predict for anyone what's going to happen. The Reiki attunement is given for eternity. It's there, in our aura, in our chakras, through life times.

I can't give you anything new. I can just show you your own light.

***

What I've learned by teaching Reiki II

Maybe I had to go far away from my parents, relatives and friends from Romania, to awaken my willingness to do distant healing. It was so liberating to find that I can still do something for them even though I am so far away.

Once learning how to use Reiki, I have healed my old wounds. Maybe not entirely, but sure enough, to the point where I am now happy, and I can live my life.

So, I am eager to share the blessings that were given to me, for all of us deserve to be happy!

Habits are powerful. The anxiety of past traumatic events can be overwhelming; it creates a false identity that defends itself from healing, and doesn't want to be healed.

In their unhappiness, some people become resentful, giving up their dreams; some complain all the time, others are drinking, or smoking, or eating compulsively, or having emotionally non-engaged sex, you name it....

We all deserve to be happy and fulfilled, but the traumas of our past will transcend through life-times and sabotage our happiness until we consciously decide to address them and heal them. In order to do so, we need to trust that it's worth being healed; we need to be willing to give up our identity of misery and pain.

To help ourselves in this process, we can make up a list of things that we would love to do as we are healed. It could be of good help to visualize movies with happy people, people who already found their way.

Being ready to allow healing and fulfillment, one could ask, "How can I heal myself?" Reiki distant healing is surely an answer. Not the only one, but one of the best.

Even when we have the tools for healing and the willingness to heal, the old identity of pain will still resist. If you're there, be aware of this and don't make yourself wrong. Instead, you could practice affirmations to support yourself through the process; if you're called to do so, create a few affirmations to sustain your purpose, print them and place them on your mirror. Here is an example:

I choose to be happy.
I choose to heal myself.
I am determined to live my best life.
I am welcoming the divine powers in my life, to heal me
and teach me, and guide me, and protect me, and remove
any old patterns that are in the way of my happiness.

***

Reiki II brings a radical change in students' lives and gives them a priceless, magical tool. Before teaching, I'm always asking the Reiki guides to use me and channel through me, talk through me, in a way that will most serve my students. Mainly I've been sharing my personal transformation with my students, but surprisingly, each time I was called to share those experiences that they could most relate to.

I am learning and teaching through Divine Love.

We are co-creators with God, and nothing should keep us from creating through the power of our spirit. So I encourage you to create new ways of using the healing tools you are given.

Practicing affirmations while looking in the mirror, after drawing the emotional symbol taught at Reiki II, is a very powerful thing. Affirmations are the fuel for maintaining ourselves on track on our journey. The Reiki emotional healing symbol connects with the subconscious mind, making the use of affirmations be more efficient.

Sei-Hei-Ki – The Reiki symbol for emotional healing

Reiki distant healing can be used for remote viewing and mediumship development.

The more we practice distant healing, the more we are able to identify the energetic imprint of people we practice on, the more we receive spiritual messages.

Becoming a medium is an imminent reward for a distant healing practitioner.

Along with the Reiki II symbols, I've been introducing all my students to a few of Shaman Manin's attunements, and especially to Flood Light, which can be used along with the distant healing Reiki. Since I took the Energetic Expansion Attunement classes with Shaman Manin before starting to teach Reiki II, all my students have been exposed to these energies and have received at least the basic information about them.

***

Once I had a Reiki II class scheduled. Even though I was fighting a cold, right before starting the class, all of a sudden, the symptoms disappeared, for the entire length of class. The presence of a higher power around me was very easy to acknowledge. My throat chakra was wide open, and a shift occurred—as if I had become a channel. I felt guided and light like a feather, in total peace. It felt like spirit was talking through me... it was magical!

The soul of my first esoteric teacher, Mr. Alexandru, was with me... and he told me through one of my friends who is communicating with souls from the other side that indeed, I was his last student on purpose—because he wanted to be connected with me and work through me after his death.

There were supposed to be four students, but one of them couldn't come that day. All day between the first three attunements given, and the fourth one, the following day, I felt so much power, it was almost painful…not necessarily their presence, but rather a cord of light.
It was like I was plugged in to the power source….Right after the last attunement given the following day, I fell asleep and didn't get up till the next day….In the morning I realized that *they* were with me for more than 24 hours because they came for my four students as a group, not as individuals. I felt like never before that we have a powerful mission together. Seeds of teamwork and spiritual partnership were planted.

When I woke up in the morning I felt the difference—it was just me...

*

Reiki II is a milestone in one's awareness about spiritual guidance. If Reiki I was bringing a sense of extra personal power, Reiki II, especially if distant healing is being practiced, gives to the new student clear evidence about the fact that he or she is not alone in the process, about the presence of spiritual guidance such as Reiki guides, spirit guides, healing guides, teacher guides, working and healing through the Reiki practitioner.

The more we practice, the more we became a channel of energy, a vehicle for spiritual healing, a connection between body, mind and spirit.

*

Wanakhavi, who had been aware of the presence of his spiritual guides prior to the Reiki II class, and who has the amazing gift of automatic writing, was encouraged to start his writing sessions now by activating all Reiki symbols, and to notice if there is an easier or more expanded communication between him and his spirit guides. Even though I had never thought this, I felt guided to tell him to draw the symbols on his throat chakra, on his writing hand and on the paper he was writing on. It seemed to help.

Hon-Sha-Ze-Sho-Nen - the Reiki symbol for distant healing and mental healing

Sue, who has been an amazing medium and spiritual healer all her life, started to give even more in-depth messages as a result of now having the distant healing symbol written in her aura. As mentioned in the Reiki handouts, this symbol connects us with the Akashic records, the book of one's soul.

*

Soon after that, I did distant Reiki on the soul of my first esoteric teacher, and he came... I felt his presence—by now I was able to identify him out of anything else. I was so happy! But my mind still didn't stay as focused as I wished it would…. And I felt his advice for me to *focus*.

Listening to my heart for what he wanted, I gave him a Reiki attunement and sent his soul two of Shaman Manin's attunements. Then I smelled the lavender pillow and a perfume for him, so he could enjoy through me. I felt so blessed to have him so "real" in my life, more than ever since he died…He left instantly at the end of the session.

I realized that as I gave my teacher, who is now in the spirit world, a Reiki attunement, I can give one to the spiritual teachers of any of my students.

From that point on, this new practice, never taught, became a very important part of my teaching.

One by one, without even planning on it in advance, this way I connected with spiritual teachers from all religious and ethnic backgrounds, through my very diverse group of students. A new door opened, toward oneness in spiritual guidance.

What a blissful experience! We are infinitely loved by God!

*

Later on, two of my best friends, Riya and Shahryar, took the Reiki classes with me. Shahryar is very psychic. When we scanned his chakras he started to see his past lives... Wow... before the attunement we meditated and I prayed to Jesus and Reiki Masters as usual to use me for giving an attunement to them and their spirit guides.... and I saw Shahryar's grandfather on his left. The way I described him was just the way Shahryar said he used to look.

About a year later, Riya was about to give birth. Three days before the big day, she asked me to give her a Reiki attunement. Her favorite God is Lord Shiva. Before starting the attunement, I prayed for a longer time with my hands on her head, asking Lord Shiva to give her now any other blessings he has for her and the baby, besides the Reiki attunement. At some point, I saw a statue of Lord Shiva in front of me. His palm was facing Riya. In his palm there was an opened eye. From that eye, a beam of light went straight to Riya's third eye, and then one went to her belly. After that, I gave Riya the Reiki attunement. Then we shared feedback and she said that right before we started, she saw light coming toward her and entering her third eye...

Three days later, a Reiki baby was born.

Through the power of the Reiki blessing before birth, the mother and her little baby girl are now enjoying an amazing telepathic connection.

This experience opened a new possibility for me: to become a Certified Doula and assist women during birth, providing them with emotional assistance and Reiki initiations for both mothers and babies, before or during birth giving.

One at a time, through my Reiki students I've been giving Reiki attunements as an offering of light to all Ascending Masters, to Lord Shiva, to Native American Guides, Jewish guides, Caribbean Guides, Egyptian Guides, grandfathers and grandmothers, beloved powerful spirits guiding and protecting them.

***

As part of the transformation process, the Reiki students are cleansing their lives—whether or not they want to—of everything that doesn't really help their spirit grow. Bob said, "You'll take on their lives," and at that point I didn't understand what he meant, but my students showed me: my responsibility is to tell them and support them in understanding that once they have a new key—the Reiki power—they are healing their past and their present, looking within and thinking twice. It's easy to get rid of everything and everyone that bothers us, but most of the time the "problem" is not outside of ourselves, but within. *Many times we are running away from people because we don't like who we are in that relationship.* Being aware of that is liberating. Sharing that is a must. We have to make sure we're doing our best before we can declare that something doesn't work.

Transformation into a true healer, into a true channel of energy, includes the healing of our emotional issues. In fact, during this process, our whole life is stirred up… and it is not easy but it is liberating at the end.

It's up to each of us, while going through the 21 days Reiki II attunement process, what do we want to take on. The Universe wants our best, we can trust that, but we have power to attract the best or not…. Live fully! Taking on healing yourself, facing any unpleasant or painful issue from your past, addressing ways of being that don't produce the results you want from your life, and not pulling yourself away from things that you have to deal with, will liberate you.

You deserve the best of <u>you</u>, and you can find the best of you, if you so choose. Be courageous! You're not alone in this.

During this process, we are often fragile, vulnerable, and even weird. We might feel the need to be in solitude, or old conflicts with the ones close to us might come to the surface. It is important that not only are the students aware of this, but also the close ones in their lives.

Communication is the key…. but yes, sometimes it is okay to stay in your cocoon for a while…. Just don't make that mean "disconnect" from your dear ones, but rather a natural step, a necessary moment in the process. A baby needs sleep to grow; it is the same here.

As we heal ourselves from any trauma from our past, we can then serve others who are going through the same experience. We can only help others heal when we are healed.

You will feel more and more the power of Reiki flowing through you, as you practice and as you go forward. It is a process, not an event. It takes time. We are creatures of habit and therefore we experience resistance to change.... Just accept it, be patient, allow yourself to be, and keep going....

After the 21 days Attunement Process for Reiki II, we have been sharing our emotional roller coaster and powerfully conclude our lessons learned. Here are a few of my students' experiences:

*karmic pain showing up—the student learned the hard way what he needed to learn, but in the process, he had experienced again old emotional traumas that came to the surface to be healed. At the end, he was liberated from attachment to painful situations, disrespectful people, and unnecessary work overload, and started to enjoy a new chapter of life, filled with ease, better opportunities and true love.

* psychic attacks during sleep—the student learned what she was meant to learn—that she is connected with divinity all the time, protected and guided, and safe.

*vivid dreams, balance, out of body experiences in her dreams, love for family; "It feels good when we are on our chart," the student said.

*lots of sleep—the student's nervous system was in the process of recovering after surgery.

*life situation bringing up old issues to be solved: "I am having a hard time already. Last night about 1:00 a.m., my husband woke me up and told me there was a fire truck and ambulance in front of our townhouse. Is it a coincidence that the last time those two vehicles showed up in front of our townhouse was the day my first husband died in our kitchen?" she asked.

"Please don't worry about the vehicles…. The only reason they were there was to tell you that you can heal a little more (I know you did a lot of work with this already) the trauma caused by your first husband's death. God bless his soul! Maybe doing Reiki on your first husband is something good for you and his spirit as well…maybe he wants you to do that…. Be Patient! Trust! You are meant to heal all this, from within out! You are infinitely loved by God! I trust you, and I trust your purpose. You'll concur yourself, step by step… it is worth doing it," I responded.

*

In the beginnings of my Reiki II teaching, I felt like I was going through a mild cleansing process myself along with my Reiki students. It was nothing like the attunement process while being a Reiki II student; it was more a learning and strengthening of spirit.

Once I was finally enjoying a quiet and peaceful afternoon, very much needed after a long week of work, studying, Reiki sessions and Reiki classes. For some reason I didn't turn my phone off, and soon, a message came as a test: "Could you please send my mom some Reiki, she's in the hospital." I felt drained, needing rest. "What do you choose—your needs or your mission?" I asked myself at first. But soon I realized that the given situation was simply acknowledging the importance of *giving the knowledge of fishing (teaching) rather than the fish (healing sessions), is reducing tremendously the moments of despair of so many people in need.*

True safety and security come from within, as we discover the tools for healing, within. So I got back to my new student's request telling him that I'll send his mom a distant healing session a couple of hours later, and in the meantime I want him to call her first and tell her how much he loves her.

Any teacher is also a student. My students have been also my teachers: through their request for support I am facing so many life situations that are teaching me and helping me to grow. My commitment to be supportive determined me to express myself in ways that were the most helpful for them. I am so very grateful! I am sharing every little step forward that I might have made, and I am so delighted to enjoy the oneness and the harmony created by having my ex-students now in my life as beloved friends and spiritual partners. I love you, dear soul-family!

Healing is love and love is healing.

***

What I've learned by teaching Reiki III

Once it is a part of people's life, Reiki supports them in accomplishing their soul mission, whatever that is. Some of my ex-students became excellent healing arts practitioners, others, better spiritual advisors, others found the love of their life, and others found their voice—their true calling. All of them have gotten great benefits out of taking the Reiki classes.

By being connected with the divine and carrying the keys of psychical healing, emotional healing, mental healing and spiritual healing within themselves, Reiki Masters become better Ambassadors of Peace, giving others hope for healing and happiness, allowing others to let their light shine too.

"We can break karma by learning the lessons" - Shaman Manin

In other words, if we learn the lessons when they are being presented to us first, we avoid further suffering. How can Reiki help us learn? By keeping us in a higher vibration and more alert, present to what happens in our life.

As a Reiki Master, the more you practice Reiki, the more you heal known and unknown wounds from your past, both from this life and from previous lives.

This is a direct result of the fact that *as you give, you receive. Eventually you heal yourself to the point where there is nothing to be triggered in you by people's problems or negative intentions.*
That's the moment when you can take your guard off and stay open, and fully be of service simply by being connected all the time at your maximum capacity with the highest powers.

Personally I've learned a lot by practicing, teaching and passing Reiki attunements, and also by taking action in the direction of my dreams, as a result of being so tuned in to the high vibration of the Reiki energy. In the first twelve months of teaching, I passed about 130 Reiki attunements, and automatically received as many.

"Giving and receiving are the same" - Gerald Jampolsky, M.D.

Passing nine Reiki Attunements within 24 hours for the first time pushed me up to the ceiling. About three days later, while meditating at night, it felt like the whole Universe opened up for me. Guidance was abundant. A new vision about life was revealed to me.

My faith in Jesus became stronger. More and more, I was calling on Jesus to work through me. My cosmic awareness expanded. The knowing about all parts of the whole Universe being connected, governed by the same simple truth, came from within. The desire of creating spiritual leaders became a true spiritual mission.

I've experienced God in a new way:

All human beings can communicate with each other through the satellite called God.

While in the past I was attached to my earthly desires, now I felt that God freed me up of anything that would disturb me from my journey. "I am ready to follow the light! I am ready to give up my life (my human desires) for the purpose of light! Jesus, please let me hear your voice! Reiki guides, guardian Angels, please open my ears and my eyes and my heart fully! *I am ready to hear, accept, allow and follow the truth.*" My body was almost floating… the connection with *all that is* felt natural, and its power was nothing else but Divine Love.

Day-Ko-Myo – the Reiki symbol for spiritual healing

The spring of life giving water is inside of you, it's your connection with God! It is in me, it is in you, it is in every<u>one</u>!

A few weeks later, Wanakhavi asked me if my vision still persists and manifests in my day by day life, if my vision was a glimpse of a different dimension of life, or the beginning of a new life. Looking, I realized that actually I still had earthly desires, but the attachment of having them has been broken. For the first time in my life, I felt that I can let go, give them up if necessary, and accept the free flow of life. On the other side, I realized that now I actually allow myself to have human experiences, without any judgment, when it feels right.

This whole experience was so much like ECKHART TOLLE's experience, described in his books, *The Power of Now* and *A New Earth*.

Looking back, observing my spiritual pathway, I saw how, for a long time, I didn't feel safe other than focusing on my spiritual life—talking, thinking, acting as such—I was afraid of getting lost otherwise in chaos, depression, bad influences, addictions, etc.... By constantly giving Reiki attunements, meditating, and giving Reiki sessions, more and more it became clear to me that I can't possibly lose my soul mission, and as a result I became more open, feeling safe in any environment, allowing myself to be human, and be of service for others as needed.

I was now able to go back and forth as I wished, and appreciate and honor everyone for where they were and who they were, and how they expressed their love. By doing so I am now able to relate with people much more than before.

Spiritual life and earthly life are joined, interconnected, interdependent and equally important!

*Earthly desires are natural. Not being attached and
addicted is all we have to be able to do.*

"So, your ego died," Wanakhavi said.

In a way, yes, but I would say that my ego became
obedient. Ego became a good servant. "I am here to
serve" is what ego now says to my spirit.

It doesn't mean that ego won't ever play games again.
Basically, as I noticed, with every significant progress
made on my spiritual journey, ego had an ugly outburst.
Perhaps this pattern will continue to manifest, but now I
am aware and I have learned what to say to please my
ego and bring it back to obedience: "Be glad to serve *this*
spirit. It has a higher purpose. Be humble. It's rewarding.
You are blessed. All is well."

As I realized many times in life, ego has its important
roles. As part of being a servant for the soul, Ego is the
alarm system of the soul. *Ego hurts to make us pay
attention and see what is to be learned.* Think about a
tooth pain. It tells us that there is an issue that needs to be
addressed and it sends us to the dentist. Same with our
ego—as we get hurt—offended, upset, nervous, angry,
afraid, insecure, etc—we should know that there is an
issue that we need to address—either a trauma that is
being triggered and needs to be healed, or something we
don't like about ourselves that could be changed (either a
way of being or a judgment, lack of acceptance, etc.).

*The most important role of our ego is to be an alarm
system for the soul.*

***

The Reiki III class includes lots of practice. Students are learning how to pass Reiki attunements, are practicing Reiki on each other, are being taught methods of protection against absorbing negative energy, and are taught about the use of crystals, pendulums, aura cleansing, and more.

With regard to ways of teaching, I've been pointing out how I'm teaching, but encouraged everyone to follow their own style. It is actually very important that a teacher listens to the voice of intuition and teaches differently from case to case according to the needs of the students.

When you're connected with the Universal Consciousness for the highest good of humanity, you don't have to worry about what you'll say or how you'll say; with Love, *allow the Universal Consciousness to talk through you, and you'll say what's most needed to be heard*, in the way it will best appeal to them. We are all already related! When you know that, how to deliver your message to others will come.

Becoming Reiki Masters means nothing more than mastering our part in the process of Reiki healing, which is to allow spiritually guided life force energy to flow through us without any constraints. Becoming a Reiki Master does not make us better than anyone else, more sophisticated or special, but rather humble and grateful for being committed channels of divine healing in the hands of God.

I'm not giving distant Reiki attunements to my students. It actually works, just as it works on the spirit of our guides or dear ones who passed away.

The spirits can see, though, but most humans don't, and therefore they doubt it. *Teachers have to enroll people in the possibility of using their gifts*, and that's what a sacred ceremony or hands on attunement is meant to do.

*

Before passing the first Reiki III attunements, I felt the presence of Spirit in a very powerful way. My crown, my throat, my heart were on fire. Very powerful! During class, we shared our learned lessons during the Reiki II attunement process, and by doing so, we taught each other, we learned from each other's spiritual journeys.

During the Reiki III attunement most students feel liberated from some sort of heaviness—they feel as if armor broke in pieces falling down and allowing them to breathe. This "armor" is actually a symbol of karmic baggage that is being healed through the power of the Reiki spiritual healing energy; it is also a reward for one's courage to take a look within and heal themselves, putting in time, energy, and a huge commitment for the highest good of humankind.

Wanakhavi was the first one to become a Reiki Master through me. Our spiritual connection had been very powerful and that gave me maximum confidence with passing the Reiki attunement. This tells once more about the fact that a teacher is also a student. It also tells about the importance of spiritual partnership and about the power of one's trust in the other's spiritual mission. My spiritual joy was infinite now knowing that he had received all spiritual tools that I was able to pass on, and knowing how much these tools can support him in accomplishing his soul mission.

My homework to assist him in his spiritual blossoming, which was revealed to me while giving him a distant healing session, was now fulfilled.

The next day, he told me that he just intended to have an automatic writing session with his guides, and none of them were there anymore. He was surprised to find that he actually now had new, more powerful spiritual guidance.

The more we move forward on our spiritual pathway, taking on more complex spiritual missions, the more powerful spiritual guidance we receive.

*

My friend Carmen received her Reiki Master attunement a few minutes before midnight on her Birthday. Right after her attunement, I had a vision with her coming out her own crown chakra. She was beautiful, grateful and joyful. It was the new Carmen, whom I love very much.

*

An interesting thing happened at the end of one of my students' attunement: I didn't want to end it for a few minutes, because of my empathy with her; during the Reiki attunement, the auras of the giver and receiver are merged, and therefore empathy is huge. At the energy level, we are basically *one*; by connecting with her pain, still not fully healed, for a moment I missed my own pain... Yes, we are attached to our own pain. I was a lot more attached till my self-healing took place, even though I wasn't aware of that.

At that time though, missing my pain only came to show me that nothing can be completely erased, but healed enough to let you live your life in peace.

*

Right after the Reiki III attunement, one of my students started to see the colors brighter. "Maybe her clairvoyance is coming back!" I thought, knowing that as a child, she used to have a high level of clairvoyance that later diminished tremendously.

Another one became more self-aware in everything she did, and forgiving herself and others, she experienced calmness and joy.

Another one had more confidence in everything he did and said, and did great work, while doing what was best for him but with consideration for others; everything was falling into place. The level of communication and acceptance shifted between him and his mom, who now loves him more than ever.

Everyone felt empowered, rejuvenated and inspired with new possibilities.

*

Below are a few affirmations for Reiki students and future Reiki students:

Reiki is Divine Love flowing through my veins.
I am a tool in God's hands.

I am connected with the Divine powers for the highest good of humanity.

I am humble and grateful; I am a light in the world

***

The more practice, the more lessons

What we first learn is just the foundation for infinite possibilities. Things evolve like a spiral of Light through the Universe…

Below are just a few examples from my own Reiki practice and what I've learned from it.

*

As soon as I received my National Certification in Massage Therapy, I started to work for a mobile spa agency, giving massages in most hotels in downtown Washington DC.

Each client has the opportunity to accept my Reiki offering, along with their requested massage. Every "yes" made my soul sing—after all, the massage school's most important outcome has been to help me open doors, giving me the opportunity to practice Reiki and other Energy Healing Techniques.

Hundreds have received Reiki along with their massage, just in my first year of practice. Every time, some new movement of hands and energy was revealed to me by my higher self and spirit guides. A new healing art modality took shape, one step at a time.

One of my most spiritually rewarding experiences as a Reiki Massage Therapist so far was with an Egyptian massage client suffering from Fibromyalgia. She accepted to try Reiki. A few minutes after we started, Nefertiti's statue came to my mind.

I thanked her for allowing me to do healing on her, which gave me the opportunity to call on the Egyptian spiritual powers and connect with them. The healing force started to flow, and the insights started to unfold. I felt that she has a great ancestry, a great spiritual gift, and that she's supposed to awaken and have a huge contribution to humanity as a result of her pursuit of health. Then I felt a motherly, feminine presence.

As I was giving her a back massage, I felt a shift, and my hands moved on her body with such deep genuine love and care, it made me wonder if I am actually channeling someone else's love. Then, I heard a voice saying, "My sweetheart, I am sorry I didn't stay with you longer." Sharing this with my client at the end of the session, she told me that her mother died when she was a teenager. She recognized her mother in my touch, as well as in the message given. This was my first experience of message channeling. It took courage to share with my client the insights I had during the massage, but it was really worth doing so—her mother's message was priceless for her.

True power of spiritual guidance is experienced when you do something for the first time, without being thought, with maximum confidence, ease, clarity and strength; when you simply know, without having the knowledge, when you are simply doing what you're guided to do, not only that you're a true channel, but new teachings for others are being born as well.

"Psychic development is not about trying to get more power, but about allowing it to unfold in your life" - Bob Hickman

*

At some point, Wanakhavi and Sue organized a Rejuvenation Fair, which was meant to provide a wide variety of healing modalities to the large public. I was so delighted to be one of the healing arts practitioners there and have an opportunity to give Reiki to so many people all day long!

That morning, before leaving my house, I looked into the purple candle for 45 minutes, praying to Jesus for the highest good of all people who would come to receive a Reiki session through me. I was calling on Jesus in a new way, and invited Him to be my Reiki Master Guide.

A Divine presence was felt by the mediums there, all day long. All sessions were great, everyone felt relaxed, peaceful, released from stress. After the first two Reiki sessions given, my intuitive channel opened, and all of a sudden I started to give each person a short message. It took some courage to speak aloud, without having any information that could support my statements, what came to mind, but I was so delighted to see that all those messages made perfect sense for each person receiving them.

What I said that day to all of the people receiving Reiki through me was that: "I am just a tool in God's hands, letting the energy flow through me; healing is between you and God."

That day I realized that I went all the way around, learning Reiki, to find a more powerful connection with my own Master Guide, Jesus Christ. Since that day, Jesus became my Reiki Master Guide.

That was the moment when, as my first Reiki teacher said, I incorporated Reiki into my religion. Whatever one's religion is, we can all do that and actually reinforce our faith.

Reiki is like a walker, till one learns to walk. Reiki is a step toward Faith Healing.

***

A Spiritual Trip to Romania

A few weeks before my already planned trip to Romania, I had an amazing dream:

I went to an old woman for a reading. That woman, though, was one of my grandmother's neighbors. She's not a medium in real life. Later on I understood that her presence led me to realize that my dream was, more than anything, a gift for my grandmother Mama Nana, who was expected to pass away at any time. The old woman was puzzled with what she'd seen in my future. So I looked at her and said, "I will die and then I will be reborn right away, isn't it?" She nodded. "Don't worry. I am not afraid," I replied.

Indeed, I was not afraid. *Fear of death disappears when we know our eternity.* Roza, my other grandmother, who died when I was fourteen, helped me learn this lesson early in life through her own example. She had strong faith, and she knew where she was going—to join Divine Light. She died with a big smile on her face, and her last words were: "I see the light." Later on, through meditation, connection with Spirit Guides and participation in Sacred Ceremonies, I have experienced my own eternity, and learned that only ego has a temporary life.

In my dream, my whole life unfolded on a theater screen, and my latest visions were all now making sense: a heart that was actually a uterus, carrying a baby, the yin/yang symbol, the messages
I've received during meditation, my self-healing and completion with my past and everyone in my life, the moments of mutually shared romantic love along my life, my traveling, my parents, my friends, my love and infinite joy for all of them... I was watching, and feeling peace, a deep state of peace, and fully accepted to die.

I got up and left my elder neighbor's house, expecting to die. Then I felt dizziness, and thought that the moment of my death had arrived. The next moment, I visualized myself in my bed. The dream continued with me trying to stand and write in my journal, which was by the bed. The pen wasn't writing. I was able to see in the room but I wasn't able to move a finger. So I started to pray: "Jesus, please help me get to the table" (where I knew that I had a pen).

"There is no death!!!!" I realized. "It's just a switch, from one dimension to another." Nothing new... but I never experienced this so clearly. Many teachings came to my mind, all saying that you don't have to die in order to find what's on the other side; you just have to imagine the feeling till you get at peace with death, while you're alive.

As I said for the third time, "Jesus, please help me get to the table," I was fully back in my body. It seemed like I was coming down from the ceiling, on a spiral, one full circle for each prayer. I was very happy for the power of my prayer during an altered state of consciousness.

Only in such altered states of consciousness can we find how powerful our faith is. Being now fully awake, I got up and tried to write in my journal by the bed, but the pen wasn't writing...just like in my dream. Then I walked to the table where there was another pen, just like in my dream, and wrote everything down.

The dream died, the reality was reborn....There are just different forms of living. My experience became a perfect analogy for the reincarnation sequence: living in the body, living in spirit, living in another body, living in spirit... day and night, day and night... No death, just different stages of consciousness.

Going further, once more I felt the importance of dying in peace. We already know that going to bed at night filled with fear, anger, worry, guilt or any other negative emotion attracts a bad night's sleep filled with nightmares or simply unpleasant dreams. Our spirit faces a web of negative entities matching our vibration and trying to take advantage of our weaknesses. The same thing happens when the soul is ready for the long journey.

My grandmother, Mama Nana, came to my mind again. "Yes, I want you to know that, and trust, there is no death but only another night coming for you, and I wish you'll go to sleep with peace and completion, with a big smile on your face, and have wonderful dreams, surrounded by Angels."

I had no idea how to help her at that point, but my love for her dying in peace stimulated once again my desire to become an effective and empowering spiritual teacher.

Not being afraid of death is freedom.

133

My heart felt deep peace and freedom, and wished that everyone can be that free.

To learn how to help Mama Nana for her long journey, right before my trip I went back to Bob for some spiritual guidance and teachings.

He told me that my grandpa's soul is already coming every day, and he'll be the one taking her and leading her to the light, but she's not aware of that. I was taught to light candles and put a glass of water in the room every day, for his soul to connect with our world. Bob encouraged me to give my grandmother a lot of Reiki, not for her body, but for her soul. He told me to connect with my grandpa, and help them connect with each other. He also said that I am indeed supposed to liberate her from the fear of death and facilitate her journey. "Show her how to look for the light. You will know what to do." Bob concluded.

***

This trip back home to Romania could have been like any other trip, except that all my relationships (with my parents, friends, and relatives) now shifted to spiritual relationships. This is one of the most powerful blessings one could ever embrace.

I was ready for my new journey. Flying overnight and seeing the sunrise from out there is one of my most desirable experiences.

Take the plane and fly above your life, be your own observer, see your own light above the clouds, and take a picture of your soul

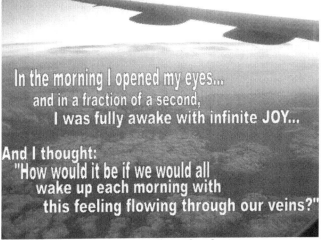

Sunrise seen from the plane

All my friends welcomed me with so much love and pure joy! Not even twenty years away would break our connection—it's so genuine and powerful!
Our time together was very short, but blissful. Two days later, my father picked me up and together we went to the village, to the house of my childhood, where my mom and my grandmother were waiting for us to get together again.

***

As I got there, my grandmother Mama Nana was almost speechless and very absent. I could see and feel her anxiety and fear, the living of an endless nightmare—the last few years of her life. I tried to make her tell me stories about my grandpa, so she would connect with him that way, but she didn't feel like talking at all.

For the moment I was discouraged and thought that it was too late. Something inside of me knew better though.... my dreams, Bob's readings....

It moved me deeply to see what a heavy duty my mom took on, by providing full care for her. Compassion can expand so much, it transcends any barriers. At the same time, it was amazing how clear my mom was—it was like a veil was lifted from her, a karmic veil. Perhaps she has fulfilled her soul mission and has learned her lessons, and she was reborn in spirit. She looked gorgeous, from the inside out.

The next day after my arrival, I gave my mom a Reiki session. It was amazing how powerfully the energy was flowing, and how intensely she was feeling it. Was it because of our powerful connection? Does the energy feel different in one's home country? So many questions... but it didn't matter; it was just so blissful to give my mom a session of divine love.

Not even ten minutes after we started, I felt the presence of my grandmother Roza's spirit. She was hugging each of us, saying, "I love you so much, my girls." Her hand of light touched mine, while I was giving Reiki to my mom. Tears of joy were falling down my face. Her presence felt so much stronger and real there, at home!

Then I gave my father a Reiki session, and again, my hands were burning so much, it was almost painful. What a miracle, to connect, hands on, through Reiki, in a more profound way, with my beloved parents... not only that I've missed them, but now it was so divine to offer a gift of light to each of them. The spiritual love I was now feeling took my breath away...

He felt it too and received it very well, but didn't let me do that again in the morning, because it made him so sleepy, he didn't have the courage to drive.

***

For the next four days, I just spent some time nurturing Mama Nana, slowly massaging her back, giving her Reiki, praying over her, massaging her hands with essential oils, and telling her how much I loved her. Slowly she started to open up and be cooperative, and answer simple questions. At night, I would tell her: "Try to remember what you've dreamed, maybe grandpa will come through."

At the end of the first day, for the first time in my life, I made a conscious effort to connect with my grandfather's soul. With the lights off, I started to simply talk to him as if he were there.... "Grandpa, it's me, Laura, your granddaughter." "Do you remember me?" "Do you remember when we were spending time together in the yard?" "Please welcome me in your house, it feels so good, it feels home!"
No answer...
"Are you here?"

No answer.... but all of a sudden I felt an impulse to go and open a drawer in the room, and when I did, a photo of him was there, right on top of everything else. Wow... communication with spirit is so subtle, so different from case to case....

"Thank you for your photo, grandpa." For the next thirty minutes, I offered Reiki light to him using his photo, through my eyes.

A candle was then lit near his photo, day and night, till I left and thereafter, till he accomplished his mission.

My grandpa, Milea, and grandma, Mama Nana, when they were young

The following night, while praying over Mama Nana, I felt the presence of grandpa's spirit, as well as the presence of my other grandmother, Roza. Learning to distinguish the energetic signature of souls is very helpful. We can all learn that without being taught how. It's enough to pay attention, to notice. Love is eternal, and infinitely powerful. Love is the vehicle toward all miracles. The more loving and powerful the connection is, the better communication flows. At that point, even though I had just identified the energetic signature of my grandpa, I felt more confident in my connection with Roza's soul. All of a sudden, an idea popped in my mind: "Grandpa, please connect with Roza, and she'll connect with me, and I'll do some Reiki on Mama Nana. This way, you'll connect better with her."

The session was great. I felt a lot of peace afterwards, and the thanks of my grandpa. Later on I learned that much more happened that night: the seeds were planted for our teamwork we've taken on in assisting Mama Nana to go to the light.

***

What an amazing and powerful thing it is to sleep in the bed of your childhood again... and reconnect with the energy of the place, and wake up in the middle of the night listening to the crickets, and then early in the morning, listening to the roosters, the goose, the dogs, the mule... and hearing Romanian voices coming from the street.

I always loved all of these blessings, but now it was even more, deeper love for everything and everyone.

Transformation comes from the inside out, and allows us to see with childish, joyful eyes the true value of the purity and simplicity of life.

My father took me to an Annual Festival about the Romanian tradition. It was so amazing to reconnect with the values I grew up with! The traditional costumes, dances, music, foods, artisan, pottery, and the purity and beauty of people's hearts!

***

My father and I also went to the cemetery to visit grandpa's grave. On our way, I blessed the pathway Mama Nana was about to follow, and her designated spot. When I told her about it afterwards, she felt lighter and very peaceful. A couple of days later, after I returned from visiting my cousins, for the first time since my arrival, we had a long conversation. It was as if she revived, to be fully awake and present, here and now. During that conversation, I shared with her my experience the day before in the Cathedral from Timisoara: after a long prayer for myself and everyone in my life, I was asking for light, and right away my body became lighter, vibrating with energy. Then, a few images crossed my mind: a cross made of light, a huge heart made of light, and two wings of light growing out of my shoulders. My story inspired Mama Nana, who now trusted more the miracles of God, the power of the Holy Spirit, and the eternal life of the soul.

She told me that she now feels ready to leave and wishes that her sister's soul would come and take her.

That was the right time for me to explain to her that her sister crossed over not too long ago and can't take on such a mission, but that grandpa will. "Let him come!" she said, for the first time being actually excited to hear about him, for the first time being connected with him. I was suddenly guided to stimulate her visualization process, and help her look for the light. She was almost completely blind, and just sometimes saw shadows, shapes, and the light of a candle.

Asking her simple questions like, "Do you remember how our goat looked?" or, "Do you remember our dog, Corbita?" her imagination, her third eye opened. She did remember.
"Do you remember the colors of her fur?" She did. She was engaged. So I put the lit candle in front of her face and said, "Open your eyes and look up." She did, and saw a huge light—the distorted way she saw it was actually so much closer to the light I was trying to help her look for. "Mama, when you're in darkness, look for this light, it's going to always be there for you. It is inside of you." The joy on her face was priceless...

***

An hour later, right before falling asleep, for the first time, deep in my heart I heard grandpa saying, "You did a good thing telling her about me." Such a subtle message... indeed we need to trust our vibes or we won't believe a word...

For the next few days, every time I was around Mama Nana, I felt my grandpa's presence. Sometimes it felt like a hug, sometimes just my hands were wrapped in gloves of light, while massaging her.

A butterfly came into the room and stayed there for a while, and I sent him light in the hope that my grandpa will receive it.

As my stay was getting close to the end, I wrote four pages of things that I loved in Mama Nana—memories from childhood, lessons she'd taught me, things that she gave me, big or little, all equally important and powerful through the grace of love.
She smiled, her face was shiny and peaceful, and she even laughed....
We said "Goodbye" in total harmony, completion and love.

Spiritual healing is of great help for the ones who are about to live as well as for the ones who are about to pass away. When a terminally ill person accepts death, they accept their destiny, they feel whole and complete, and they feel peace in their heart, detachment and love. It can only be a gift to feel that way, even though they might actually live longer.

***

During my last night spent in my room, I observed myself during my soul's short journey for the first time, going through the walls, flying high, seeing my body resting in the bed, and coming back.... A true out of body experience, in the presence of my family, in the home, the room, the bed of my childhood... the more we go forward on our spiritual journey, the deeper are the meanings of "feeling home." We're going outward and inward at the same time.

As I left, and said goodbye to my parents, for the first time I knew that one day I'll spend more time with them again, there, and it's not going to be something I'll have to do, but a true honor, pleasure and delight. It will impact many other people around in a very good way. It's a faraway dream, but the seeds are there, and the feelings of love, total acceptance, harmony, completion, compassion and joy will find a way when the time will come.

***

My cousin Tiberiu picked me up from the train station in Timisoara. Our joy to see each other again was beyond words.
We stopped in the park and watched the sunrise in stillness, connecting with Divine Light, and with each other's soul.

Then we went over his place, and he was playing guitar – a song he composed that moved me so deeply—tears were falling down my face.

O, brother, our souls are connected through eons! I'm looking at you and I see through centuries of lives...I am so blessed to see you again....

My life in the United States is so beautiful... I've integrated, made true friends, spiritual friends from all over the world, it is home for me now... but when I see you, everything else seems so new... our souls met so long ago, since the beginnings...

What are we meant to create and accomplish in this life together? In divine time, we will find the answer. But for now, just being pure love for each other is a true source of life; it's a flowing fountain of life-giving water.

That day, for the first time, I connected in a spiritual way with my other cousin, Lucian. I was fascinated to discover what an amazing spiritual being he is, how powerful he is....God, we are so very blessed!

We visited Timisoara, a beautiful city, and had a blast.

Then we went on a journey together, and it was out of this world. It felt as if we were traveling through tunnels of time, and everything was possible through our sustainability.

We stopped to visit the ruins of a 1900-year-old city, the first one built by Romans on the land of our ancestors, in the year 110.

The energy of that place was so powerful, the connection was so old... it lifted our spirits so much...

When we arrived at his parents' house, we meditated together and light was being poured all over us by our spirit guides and Angels, and then we were bursting into a flowing fountain of light, higher, and higher... out there in the Universe.

Than we said goodbye till next time...

***

Tiberiu's mom, Vali, and her sister Mimi, are both Reiki Masters. Wonderful souls, wonderful healers! They were not taught how to pass Reiki attunements, and were very willing to be empowered to do so. Therefore, we got together and shared with each other our spiritual journeys, lessons we've learned, tips and little secrets, and moreover, our hearts.

It is so important to have at least one person in your life that you can mirror with, that you can work with, practice with. Empowering each other on a regular basis is the secret of continuous spiritual growth.

We learned by doing. So, I gave a Reiki attunement to Vali first, and then Vali watched me doing the same thing for Mimi. She took a photo, but didn't realize what came up in it. Then, they gave each other Reiki attunements, while I was leading them through the process.

Adding the Reiki attunements connection on top of our existing connection was a very blissful experience. A transformed life is one filled with oneness, is one of sharing and expanding Divine Light.

At night, when I got home and downloaded the photos, I was astonished to see that a white horse appeared in the photo she took, a horse made out of the incense's smoke. The soul of my first esoteric teacher, Alexandru E. Russu, had enough power there in Romania to materialize in a symbol that made sense to me, and show himself to me and anyone else, while guiding me and working through me. Thank you, my dear teacher, so very much, for always being with me while doing light work. I am grateful and humbled looking up to you, and I love you so very much, now and always!

White horse materialized from smoke while giving a Reiki attunement

Ever since, Mimi and Vali have been offering each other this beautiful gift of light any time they wanted.
The seeds were growing into two powerful flowers, which can now expand into a beautiful garden.

It was so delightful to hear, maybe six months later, that they started to give Reiki attunements.

***

My friends, Geny and Paul, took me on a magical trip in the Bucegi Mountains. We went to a beautiful place, called Padina, which is known to be a mystical spot, a powerful ancient energy vortex.

Getting closer and closer, we were feeling the perfection of nature and God more and more. Such a peace, fresh air, quietness and harmony! We were all waiting for something magic to happen. We saw the mountain's aura, the grid of light, colorful stars, and sometimes a vortex of light.

At some point, Geny asked Paul to stop the car. She was called by her higher self to go to a certain spot by the creek, down the road. She walked for less than three minutes till she found it.

There was a little wooden bridge to help people cross to the other side of the creek. Maybe it was a bridge toward another dimension of life....The waterfall was so peaceful, the rays of the sun so gentle, and the trees so old....

She received a Reiki attunement right there, in that place of Heaven. We were holding hands in a sacred union, grasping our new, deeper spiritual connection.

*

147

About an hour later we arrived at the cavern of our ancestors. I'm calling it that way because Decebal, the last king of our ancestors, used to go there on a regular basis, perhaps to charge himself energetically before battles. The name of this wonderful and magical place is Pestera Ialomicioarei.

At the entrance, there is a monastery and a beautiful gate.

As soon as I stepped through the gate, I felt called to go straight to a particular spot, sit down and meditate. The energy was different than any other place. It felt like a whole new Universe unfolded there, as if the cavern was the door to a parallel world.

A spiritually gifted person who saw me, asked me later: "Did you know what you've done?" "No, please tell me," I responded. "You opened a gate; there were many spirits with you, including the spirit of Zamolxes (the God of Romania's ancestors); come back tomorrow and you'll see." He also told us where can we find a room—we had not made any reservations. He was like a messenger sent from God.

Next morning we went back, and as we entered into the cavern, we prayed for the spirits of our ancestors, and asked them to welcome us in their house. Along the way, I drew the Reiki symbols on the walls of the cavern and took many pictures of amazing shapes on the walls. With my forehead touching the rocks, I prayed to God to allow us to see the spirits of our ancestors.

For a while, it seemed like I was talking to the walls...
but then, I saw a huge rock looking like a head and neck
of a white horse. My heart started to beat faster. "The
spirit of my esoteric teacher announces to me about
something," I thought. Right away, I took my camera out
and started to take photos of a place near that rock
formation. After the first click, for a fraction of a second,
I saw steam in the photo. Looking with the physical eyes,
the steam couldn't be seen. I took one more picture and
again, on the screen of the camera, something like steam
was covering the whole surface, but again, nothing
different for the physical eyes. The third photo taken was
clear.

At night, we were shocked downloading the photos in the
computer, to see that there were shapes of spirits and
many overlapped spiritual beings in those two photos.
One of the clearest two shapes looked like Jesus on the
cross, and the other one, like the profile of Decebal, the
last king of our ancestors.

Spirit photographed in Ialomicioara Cavern, Romania

What an honor, to be shown the spirits of our ancestors! We were grateful and humbled.

Before we left the cavern, a drop of water fell on the top of my head... and I stopped, and waited for more, till seven drops "baptized" me. Then I received one in each palm.... Wow, what a gift... total peace, harmony and oneness. Thank you, God!

We left the cavern and went up on the highest peak, to visit natural landmarks—rocks shaped naturally by wind. We felt as if we were outside of time... and then we realized that *the crown chakra has no age, and by living tuned into our connection with divinity, everything seemed timeless*... the spiritual bliss is eternal, old, and so we felt as if we had been there forever....

***

As we enjoyed seeing the natural landmarks called Babele and Sfinxul, up there on the mountains at 6000 feet, now we decided to enjoy a three hour hike going down, back to our hotel. We chose to ignore the trail and go straight in the median line cutting through a huge triangle formed by Babele, Sfinxul and Pestera Ialomicioarei. On the route we took, it is said that there is a powerful energy vortex.

We were all quiet and profoundly tuned into the high vibration of the place. At some point, my higher self said, "Sit down here," and in the very next moment, Geny said, "Let's sit down here." We both felt that there was something different, something we wanted to experience, something we were guided to pay attention to.

That was the place were Geny and Paul received their Reiki Master attunement. I prayed for our ancestors and for the spirit of that magical place, to receive the attunement as well, as an offering of light, and as a result, to connect even deeper with the mystical place, with the mountains, with the ancient spirits living there. In the photos taken, at the end of the Reiki attunements, our auras could be seen, especially around our heads.

Afterwards we lay down on the grass for a few minutes, to grasp the majestic moment, and right then a vulture flew right above us...
Visualizing that I melted and merged with the mountain, green grass grew over me and sheep walked over me...
Roots were growing out of me deep into the mountain; the roots of my spirit, and a pure, profound spiritual joy took me over and guided me through the magnificence of the moment.

We continued our journey together, speechless, in total wholeness, harmony and peace. As we were getting to the end of our stay, Geny stopped us again, for the third time, in another magical place filled with an incredible, different kind of energy—very feminine, like a crystalline loving laughter... She saw a huge violet globe of light above the peaks of the mountains, and then we all saw a rainbow, symbolizing the Goddess energy.

Soon we said "Goodbye" till next time...

***

On the plane, reading my mom's poetry, I was so impressed, and so amazed at her wisdom, mystical knowing, magical metaphors, true love.... tears were falling down my face... tears of joy, spiritual joy, infinite love....While reading about her father, Stefan, whom I've never met (he passed away when my mom was young) I connected with him like never before. Seeing how profound his faith in God was, seeing what a golden heart he had, I welcomed him into my life, in my spiritual life, and ever since, prayed for him just as I do for the other members of the family who passed away. I felt a complete circle closing, moving like a spiral toward the light.

Just a few days later, I woke up in the morning laughing out loud.... it never happened to me before.... what was I dreaming—I couldn't remember.... but what I did remember later that day, was my mom telling me how her father, Stefan, used to laugh in his sleep... Oh, my God, he really heard the calling of my heart, and came in my dream giving me a sign... How amazing and wonderful!

My heart was filled with love and gratefulness. A new beginning, a new stage of life, was ready to unfold.

Did you ever wonder how much more is available for us out of any experience, any relationship, any trip... when we fully open our heart for true love?

***

A New Soul Mission

For many years, I used to make lists of goals at the beginning of each year, and prayed to God for the help and support needed to accomplish everything. Some of my goals were very material and earthly; others were more aligned with my soul mission.

The event described below had not been on my list of goals, yet, as it happened, it represented a huge accomplishment to me, defining a new soul mission.

I understood the importance of inviting, allowing and embracing God's goals for me. Even my prayers in the beginning of the year have changed: *God, all is possible with your help. Please help me fulfill all that is aligned with my soul mission on my list of goals below. Please reveal new soul missions to me, and help me accomplish everything you want me to do. I am so delighted to receive all the blessings that you and the Universe have to give me!*

***

Reiki Attunement during sleep before my grandmother's death

It was Tuesday morning when I woke up from this amazing dream: my luminous body was in Romania, in my grandmother's room.

I was doing Reiki on her, and untying her links with this world (it was like I was undoing braids). There was just one I couldn't release her from, deep under the skin. Praying to Jesus in the most profound way, I said: "Jesus, only you can do that" (untie her). Then I went in front of her and gave her a Reiki attunement (initiation, empowerment). I was drawing the Reiki symbols in front of her, as big as her body. At the end, she looked at me and said, peacefully: "I'm ready, take me." "Take" was in the plural, as if she knew that there were more beings there with me (the Reiki Guides).

I woke up, got up, took her picture between my hands and did Reiki again…. But it was early in the morning and I was somewhere between sleep and reality… and I was sent back there… just my luminous body, again, was floating in her room, close to the ceiling, and I was holding hands of light with my grandfather (her husband, who passed over 30 years ago) and my other grandmother (who passed over 20 years ago), and another three light beings. We were all dancing in a circle above her head, looking down toward her, and I wasn't sure if she was still alive or not. Then I said, "Jesus, please fill this room with Light," and it poured Light all over…. And then beautiful hearts of light started to float in the room…and then I got back fully in my body, in my room.

She died three days later.

Afterwards, my mom told me that since that Tuesday, she shifted all of a sudden to a state of profound peace, and her face was full of light till she died... Moreover, that day my mom heard Mama Nana calling grandpa's name, and saying: "I'm ready, take me."

I have chills as I'm writing this story. Maybe she's here with me right now.... I am so grateful to God! I am so grateful to Jesus! He helped her un-tie the thick rope... Along my life I never saw Mama Nana as being a spiritual partner but now I know that she knows that it is all true....and we love each other truly, at the spiritual level.

God bless Mama Nana's soul!

Imagination and psychic experiences are always combined and you never know for sure how much of each is what... but who cares? Don't even try to figure it all out. The most important is the *love* that you give and the connection that you keep alive.

This very special event in my life opened up for me *a new soul-mission: to offer Reiki attunements to people who are terminally ill, for the purpose of spiritual healing, and to ease soul's journey toward the light.* It was not one of my goals, but much more important than our own goals are God's goals for us to accomplish.

For the next 40 days, I was praying and sending Reiki to my grandmother every day, and sometimes I had small conversations with her... very simple ones—I just asked simple questions like, "Do you like Reiki?" "Can you see the light?" "Are you with grandpa?" "I love you" "Use this candle's light" etc.... and I felt her loving, somehow childish voice answering in her own words.

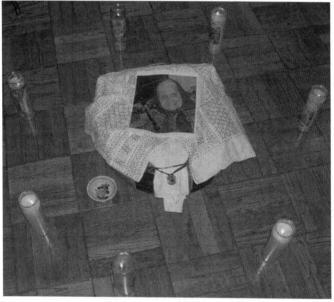

A photo of Mama Nana, placed on a hand made traditional shirt she had made in the 1920s, at the age of 13, surrounded by seven lit candles.

In my life-transforming teenage dream, revealing the colorful stars entering into the Holy Cross, it was the time of my grandmother's death... and yet, this was the time when the union between healing and faith took a higher step forward for me.

All spiritual gifts are being reopened by serving humanity: out of body experience being on a mission, hearing, remote viewing, being a vessel for healing and liberation from the fear of death.

Any blessing I've prayed for came with homework, a very meaningful one. Thank you, God!

Since my grandmother's death, I've been giving many other offerings of light right before or right after different people's death. Reiki attunements are always part of the process.

Here is the sequence:

1. Cut cords (the attachments with this world)
2. Give a Reiki attunement
3. Run the White Cross attunement provided by Shaman Manin and Councils

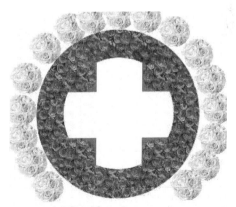

White Cross Attunement

The White Cross attunement - by Shaman Manin

Every time, I'm allowed to have a vision that would give me a specific message for that particular case. I've been learning so much out of these experiences.... What a blessing to serve God and to be taught by spirit!

Many cases and the lessons learned are presented in my book entitled *Focused on Spirit*.

To give my life to God took a new meaning: *being a tool in God's hands doesn't have to mean giving up an earthly existence, including a mundane life, a family, children and a regular job. It could simply mean listening to God, and using the current life circumstances to develop new soul missions.*

***

Our Reiki Family

We are talking with each other from the heart. We trust each other. We offer each other support during life challenges, with good words, good thoughts, distant healing, prayers, and especially, through our unconditional love for each other.

Once I sent healing light to one of my friends who had a hard day, and later that day asked him if he felt anything. He said "No, but I know that your love is always there."

*

I remember what a huge effort Wanakhavi made to set up a Rejuvenation Fair, while he was in the middle of so many other things.... and I remember when I told him that he will be rewarded... not by the host of the event—but by the Universe.... and he met Whitney, such an amazing woman who became an incredible spiritual partner and friend. The three of us had weekly spiritual gatherings and had metaphysical conversations for a long time.

*

As Reiki practitioners, we partner with divine powers, we merge into Universal Consciousness, and so the nature of our thoughts, concerns, feelings and habits changes.

We started to organize Reiki Reunions, and give each other Reiki attunements for the purpose of keeping each other in a high vibration.

Everyone who has ever received a Reiki attunement can feel a drop in their energy at the end of a 21 days attunement process. It manifest in many ways, sometimes by going back to thought patterns that are not as positive, sometimes by boredom, lack of motivation and determination, less energy, optimism, desire to give and more. Once having this wonderful spiritual tool—the Reiki attunements, why not keep each other for most of the time in a higher frequency?

For the new Reiki Masters this is also an opportunity to learn and practice passing Reiki attunements.

My stand for all Reiki Masters is to be confident passing Reiki attunements, whether or not they'll ever teach. Learning from experience that Reiki attunements can help a dear soul in their transition toward the light, as well as connect with spirit guides, with my grandmothers and grandfathers, I realized that becoming a Reiki Master/Teacher is a priceless gift that can be used in so many other ways anyway. Sharing and assuring that each of us has these gifts at their convenience has been a pleasure and delight.

*

Shelley is one of my dear friends who became a Reiki Master. Below is her feedback about her first Reiki Reunion:

"I became a Reiki Master less than a month ago, after an emotionally difficult 21-day attunement process. At the end of the 21 days, I felt empowered and ready to start using my new energy, but wasn't sure how to begin.

When Laura invited me to a Reiki fair, I wanted to attend, but was intimidated. Reiki sounded great in theory, but did I really have the tools to help someone?

"The person whom I worked on agreed to be my 'guinea pig' and was patient. I was amazed to feel the healing energy flow through my body and by the sudden intuitive insights that flashed through my mind. I suddenly realized that the person I was working on had a knee issue, though he hadn't told me and there was no logical way that I could know this. When I asked, he confirmed that this was indeed the case. Wow!

"After the healing session was over, I observed an attunement and received one (which felt amazing; it was worth going for the attunement alone)! Then I had the chance to perform attunements on two other Reiki Masters. I made a lot of mistakes in the process, but am glad to have made them. After all, it's only by making mistakes that we grow."

"Your talent is God's gift to you. What you do with it is your gift back to God." ~Benton's mom (from the TV show ER, in reference to healing)

*

Our Reiki Reunions have been absolutely delightful. We are having so much fun, we're sharing wonderful thoughts, and we play drums together and practice on each other new healing arts we might have been learning. Some of us, who have discovered their mediumship abilities, give spiritual messages, automatic writing sessions or channeling and healing sessions.

Sometimes we take our gifts out there in the world for others, serving as healers at Rejuvenation Fairs and Sacred Festivals.

Sue and Wanakhavi have made a great effort to organize Rejuvenation Fairs. More and more of us—the Reiki Masters—started to offer Reiki sessions to the large public.

Graciela, the youngest Reiki Master of our group, was one of the main organizers of the Sacred DC Festival. She gave all of us the opportunity of practicing Reiki on so many people attending the festival, including children.

Shahryar is my dear life-long friend. Bob confirmed my vibes regarding our past-life connection and said that we were working in Egyptian temples together in a past life and supported each other through our entire life. Shahryar loves children very much, and he gives them all his love through colorful gemstones, attuned with the Reiki energy. For my delight, he did that once at the Sacred DC festival, on Father's Day, inside my copper pyramid.

Love and light goes around in circles. Thanks to Terri, who encouraged Wanakhavi to sign up on meetup.com, I met Wanakhavi; a year later, Carol, whom I knew from a different Reiki group, joined us. As Carol and Terri met, they became best friends and spiritual partners right away. I was so delighted to see them giving Reiki together to the Sacred Festival attendants.

*

Sometimes Spirit shows us its amazing way of connecting and working through us. Here is an example:

We scheduled a Reiki Reunion. One of the Reiki Masters, who lives farther away than anyone in the group, really wanted to practice giving Reiki attunements, but decided to do that on a Teddy Bear at home, with the intent of sending me the attunement. Her name is Ana. She didn't call us and none of us was aware about her doing that. In the meantime, I was passing a Reiki attunement to Carol. In the Reiki attunement process, there is always a divine presence or a Reiki Guide who's using the giver's body to actually give the attunement. The giver is simply performing a ritual, letting the Life Force Energy flow freely through.

So, Carol received a Reiki attunement through me, from a Reiki Guide or spirit guide that could have been, as usual, anonymous. Right after receiving the Reiki attunement, she asked Wanakhavi for an automatic writing session. He started to communicate with a spirit, who revealed herself as being the Reiki Guide who just gave Carol the Reiki attunement through me.

Wanakhavi was writing almost a page for Carol, as the words of a true Reiki Teacher were coming through. Wanakhavi then asked what her name is, and she wrote "Ana." "Do you mean Ana—our Ana?" he asked. "Yes," the answer came, over and over again. We couldn't believe it, but Wanakhavi knew deep in his heart that it was true. Personally I had never heard till that point about such a story, and wondered if Ana was aware of the fact that she was giving a remote Reiki attunement.

163

A week later, to our surprise, the four of us met at church, and Ana came to tell us about how she passed a Reiki Attunement for me through the Teddy Bear, and then, all of a sudden she became very sleepy and went to bed. Then we realized that I was passing the Reiki attunement to Carol right in the moment when I was actually receiving one from Ana. Then while Ana went to sleep, she had an out of body experience and her spirit communicated with Carol through Wanakhavi.

We were amazed to see how the higher powers are working through us as a group, strengthening the depth of our spiritual connection.

*

Some of us gather every other week for meditation. Together, as Reiki Masters and Energy healers, we are letting the Reiki energy flow freely in the meditation circle, for all our new meditation group members to experience.

Carrie and Miguel, an amazing couple whom everyone loves very much, are very often leading the meditation. Sometimes new members of the group are sharing their favorite meditation techniques. Sometimes we are just simply holding hands listening to the drums, in the Meridian Hill (Malcolm X) Park, in the core of Washington DC.

Before our first meditation circle in the park, Carrie and I drew the Reiki symbols on our hands, to let the Reiki energy flow freely during our meditation.

Then we all visualized a column of diamonds behind each of us; the energy circulating between the diamonds created a protective circle of light. We started our meditation session, quietly holding hands. Running the energy expansion attunements taught by my teacher, Shaman Manin, visualizing all Reiki symbols flowing through each of our auras, visualizing an Angel pouring light on each of our heads, and the current of light flowing in circles from one to the next, hearing the drums, connecting with the Earth, surrounded by nature, we had an amazing spiritual experience.

We all received a healing and emotionally releasing Reiki session as well, by letting the Reiki energy flow in the circle. Some of us were also holding gem stones that are part of my personal chakra stone set; these gem stones have received hundreds of Reiki attunements and are being of service while doing light work.

When Ruth joined us, the circle became whole, because of her and Brett's wholeness, through love. I felt a shift instantly. As soon as she started to hold hands with us, the spirit of the forest/nature came into my vision, waving white wings of light, dancing in the middle of our circle. How magical and serene!

Once I didn't focus on sending any energy sequences in the circle, just prayed to God and to the Reiki guides to "let us, your beloved children experience your light." And we did! It was amazing…a girl's smile… She switched from questioning to joy…Thank you, God and beloved Spiritual Guides!

*

165

Leigh, a dear coworker and good friend, has been a source of inspiration for me in many ways. Just by being such a wonderful family man, a loving husband and a loving father who would do anything for his children, he has unconsciously nurtured my hope of one day having my own "loving family..." Through limited interaction at work, just by sharing the office and work projects, I consider him to be one of my lifelong spiritual partners. The nickname I gave to Leigh is "Happy Daddy," since his love and sense of obligation toward his children serves as a genuine source of "energy" for him to strive to accomplish great things in his life. It brought joy to my heart when Leigh decided to become a member of my Reiki Family as well. Knowing what a blessing he is to the people he comes in contact with on a daily basis, I am excited to see what good he will do in the world through the power of Reiki.

*

My friend Carmen is an amazing jewelry designer. With dedication to her art, since she became a Reiki Master, Carmen transfers her love, passion and Reiki energy on to her jewelry. Copper has been used for jewelry and as a means of improving health perhaps since man first discovered it. The use of wire goes back to ancient times. Ancient Egyptians wove pieces of wire jewelry, as did the Chinese in their intricate filigree. It can be said that wire is alive.

*

Our Reiki Family gets bigger and bigger… and is just one of many others. Nowadays there are thousands of Reiki Masters all over the world, and so many other Energy Healers and Teachers whose level of spiritual development, faith and healing abilities are making a great impact for the world and our planet.

A while back, Bob, my spiritual consultant, told me that my last words spoken before my last "death" were: "I will return and I will heal the world." Day by day, it is being revealed how that could be possible: through oneness, through *you*! Teaching Reiki, Psychic Development and Shamanic practices, supporting people from a wide variety of professions, all cultural, religious and ethnic backgrounds on their spiritual journey is the way to spread the most seeds of light.

So, it is not me, who has to heal the world.

"Who's healing the world?" one might ask.

The answer is:

You, loving mothers!

You, loving fathers!

You, loving grandparents!

You, loving nannies, doulas and midwives!

You, loving children!

You, loving nurses, doctors and Emergency personnel!

You, loving writers!

You, loving lawyers!

You, loving food servers!

You, loving farmers!

You, loving teachers!

You, loving politicians!

You, loving professionals!

You, loving taxi drivers!

You, loving scientists!

You....

You, loving spiritual beings, by opening your hearts and your minds,

Allowing the divine healing and the Universal Consciousness to flow through you,

For your highest good and the highest good of all that is!

*

"We change the world not by what we say or do, but as a consequence of what we have become."
- David R. Hawkins: Psychiatrist, spiritual author, and lecturer

Tools for Energy Healers

Reminders for our inner healer

Being committed to become a healer comes with the obligation of self-healing.

Our physical bodies are temples of God. We need to respect and honor them, and treat everything —our spiritual life and physical life—as being equally important. We were sent to Earth in a body for a reason. Trusting God and accepting God's mission for us includes honoring our physical bodies.

Trusting God means accepting things that happen to us even without understanding. The other way around faces the failure of understanding all the time, and as a result, we suffer. Accepting what happened even without understanding is a measurement of one's faith in God, and it's key in one's happiness.

We can remove any barrier or thought pattern that stays in the way of our happiness and success. If we don't know what it is, we can always ask for divine help.

*Let's look within for our power, not outside of ourselves;
let's look within for our faith, not outside of ourselves;
let's look within for miracles, healing, love and light, not
outside of ourselves; let's look within for God! There is
no miracle that can be given to us, because it is in us
already; only the key to unlock the power of love inside of
us can be given through teachings and healing.*

*Healing is love and love is healing. As we learn to love
ourselves and all, we experience oneness, and as we
experience oneness, we find peace. As healers, we are
Ambassadors of Peace.*

*Healing brings love, love brings peace, and peace brings
oneness.*

*The Healing Force and the Universal Consciousness are
flowing together, they are one!*

*If God wants us to serve Him, He'll give us the power to
do so.*

*As healers, we don't give from us, we give through us. We
are but vessels of Spiritually Guided Life Force Energy;
the fewer blockages in our body-mind-spirit, the better
vessels we become.*

*As healers we have to find the balance between being
loving and being detached. Allowing God to work
through us requires a God-like attitude. In the eyes of
God, all is well.*

*As healers we must be humble. All our gifts would not
have unfolded for us and the ones we serve, without
God's will.*

Our ego is the one who suffers. Our soul is always whole, perfect and complete. Therefore, all suffering is nothing but delusion.

The most important role of our ego is to be an alarm system for the soul.

Ego becomes our servant. "I am here to serve" is what ego gets to say to our spirit.

Fear of death disappears when we know our eternity.

Enlightenment is a direct result of self-healing. Our wounds are a heavy metallic armor. As the armor breaks, our light within can shine.

Enlightenment means to be focused on light: the light of our spirit, the light of spirit.

Reiki is Divine Love flowing through the veins of the healer.

Reiki is like a walker, till one learns to walk. Reiki is a step toward Faith Healing.

Reiki is not only a tool for healing, but also for enlightenment and psychic development. Becoming a Reiki Master and being able to give/receive Reiki attunements is priceless, and it can be used in many ways: to keep ourselves and other Reiki Masters in a continuous high vibration; to offer gifts of Light to our ancestors, grandparents, dear ones who passed away, to our Spiritual Guides, and more.

Our pure hearts make us raw healers. Training makes us professional healers. Sharing makes us spiritual teachers.

Note: If you feel the calling to have Reiki as a tool of enlightenment and healing in your life, this book contains all you need to know about Reiki. Throughout the chapters of this book are many examples of how to use Reiki. At the end of the book, you have the most specialized Reiki knowledge (the Reiki symbols, how to pass a Reiki attunement, how to protect yourself and more). All you need is to receive the Reiki attunements from a Reiki Master and to practice as much as possible.

Reiki Students' handout

(Credit given to: Samantha Beathy's *Reiki Handouts*, Shaman Manin's *Reiki Handouts*; *Chakra Healing* – Rosalyn Bruyere; *The Chakra Energy Plan* – Anna Selby).

In addition to all the Reiki stories in this book, below is the essence of the Reiki Teachings, the information that Reiki Students need to learn as part of their Reiki class. Don't forget, though, to become a Reiki Practitioner and ultimately a Reiki Master you must receive the Reiki attunements from a Reiki Master. This book serves as Reiki Handout and I encourage you to read it once prior to/during your Reiki training.

The chakras

Chakra # 1 & associated color: Root/Muladhara/ Red

Name meaning: root & support
Quote: "I trust my body and I trust its wisdom"
Symbolizes/ Focus: Life, vitality, strength and physical nature of man; just is / Survival and physical security
Sense: Smell
Endocrine gland: Adrenals

Health/Healing: Spinal column, colon, legs and bones, anxiety, grounding, addictions, fear, pain, colitis, diarrhea, abortion/miscarriage recovery, menopause, moving forward, karma, death, reincarnation, past lives, uterus, menstruation, fertility, life force, red blood, circulation, warmth, constipation, AIDS, leukemia, cancer
Location: Base of spine; here is the Kundalini energy; when this reaches the crown we get bliss and enlightenment
Element: Earth
Age like personality: 4
To balance it: A good massage stimulates root chakra.
Well balanced personality: Creating your stability, caring, strong, healing, compassionate, knows when to fight and when to let go (choose the battles)
Out of balance personality: The victim; low self-esteem, addictive behavior, out of touch with the body and with sexuality
Oils and Incenses: Lavender, Cedar, Patchouli
Gemstones: Bloodstone, red jasper, smoky court, Red Tiger's Eye, robin, moss agate

***

Chakra # 2 & associated color: Sacral/ Svadhistana / Orange

Name meaning: that which belongs to itself
Quote: "I deserve pleasure in my life"

Symbolizes/ Focus: Energy; a combination of red=personality and yellow=wisdom; just feels; feeling and caring for self (how this will make me feel) / Emotions, sexuality, procreation, color, design, taste, sexual awareness (not primal sexual drive)
Sense: Taste
Endocrine Gland: Gonads
Health/Healing: Ovaries/testicles, prostate, genitals, womb and bladder, sexuality, orgasm, fertility, menstruation, ovarian cysts, endometriosis, asthma, allergies, epilepsy, arthritis, impressions, visualization, spleen, coughs, all body fluids
Location: Few inches below the Navel
Element: Water
To balance it: Swimming, Jacuzzi, long showers, arts, Lymphatic Drainage
Age like personality: 7
Well balanced personality: Graceful, friendly, communicative, trusting, in touch with friends, optimistic, self-expressed
Out of balance personality: The murderer; guilt, self-pity, manipulative, envy, disregard for sexual partners
Oils and Incenses: Rosemary and Amber
Gemstones: Carnelian, Orange calcite, Fluorite, Orange Topaz

***

Chakra #3 & associated color: Solar plexus/ Manipura / Yellow

Name meaning: city of jewels

Quote: "I can do whatever I will to do"
Symbolizes/ Focus: intellect, mind, high intelligence and wisdom; just thinks; thinks based on past experiences, on what you already know/ Will, purpose, power, self-empowerment, self-honor
Sense: See
Endocrine Gland: Pancreas
Health/Healing: stomach, liver, pancreas, diabetes, digestion, eating disorders, ulcers, urinary, muscles and the nervous system, assimilation, nutrition, ideas, energy, psychic, apathy, tiredness, will power, visualization, depression.
Location: between the chest and the Navel
Element: Fire
Age like personality: 12
To balance it: Fasting and avoiding snacking balances this chakra.
Well balanced personality: Spiritual warrior, belief in something bigger than you, inner strength, integrity, strong will-power, courageous
Out of balance personality: The judge, irresponsible (I did that because you did that), fearful, guilty
Oils and Incenses: Rose and ylang-ylang
Gemstones: Amber, Citrine, moonstone

***

Chakra #4 & associated color: Heart/ Anahata/ Green

Name meaning: Unbeaten
Quote: "I am worthy of love"

Symbolizes/ Focus: Harmony, creativity, health, abundance and nature; cares for others; it is the combining of yellow (soul) and blue (spirit) / Love, compassion, forgiveness of others and yourself, self love
Sense: Touch
Endocrine Gland: Thymus
Health/Healing: immune/thymus, infections, heart/heart disease, blood circulation, circulatory system, arms and lungs, love, loneliness, self-image, trust, abused childhoods, giving, compassion, receiving love, imagination
Location: Center of chest
Element: Air
Age like personality: 18
To balance it: A gentle massage stimulates it.
Well balanced personality: The lover: give and receive unconditionally and equally; fulfilling hopes and dreams, energized
Out of balance personality: The performer (sabotage, gossip), unable to let go of fear, lack of confidence.
Oils and Incenses: Rose, Lavender, Jasmine
Gemstones: Aventurine, Sapphire, Jade, Rose Quartz

***

Chakra #5 & associated color: Throat/ Visuddha / Blue

Name meaning: Pure
Quote: "I hear and speak the truth"

Symbolizes/ Focus: inspiration, devotion, infinity and religious goals; produces calm and peace; controls the tone of your voice; communication, self expression, listening, sound, vibration
Sense: Hear
Endocrine Gland: Thyroid
Health/Healing: Thyroid, throat and mouth, voice burns, sore throats, laryngitis, choking, headaches, migraines, inflammations, swelling, ears, anger, rape and incest recovery, communication, self-expression, creativity.
Location: Throat
Element: Ether
Age like personality: 35
To balance it: Singing and Mantra during meditation stimulates it.
Well balanced personality: the good communicator
Out of balance personality: inappropriate, disrupt the class and make everything about them, fake
Oils and Incenses: Lavender and Hyacinth
Gemstones: Turquoise, Lapis Lazuli, Aquamarine, Sapphire, Blue Agate

***

Chakra #6 & associated color: Third eye/ Ajna / Indigo or light Purple

Name meaning: Command
Quote: "I trust my inner vision and intuition"

Symbolizes/ Focus: Spiritual attainment, self mastering and wisdom; it aids in the opening of the third eye—inner and outer vision—and opens the doors to subconscious; seeing, visualization, clairvoyance, light, psychic perception, intuition, imagination, emotional intelligence, seeing and believing that that you can't touch;
Sense: Sixth sense
Endocrine gland: Pituitary
Health/Healing: Pituitary & pineal gland, nose, ears and left eye, endocrine balancing, menstrual cycles, pneumonia, senses, multiple sclerosis, headaches, degenerative diseases, white blood cells, immune system, colds, flu, sinuses, mental and psychic development, clairvoyance.
Location: above and between the eyes
Element: Radium
Age like personality: 46-52
To stimulate it: Focused eye and Mind, and use of affirmations stimulate it, time in nature.
Well balanced personality: The Psychic; respect and privacy for other people; will command you with no excuse to do what you want to do; a sense of divine in all things, a sense of completion and being *one* with all creation.
Out of balance personality: The rationalist—need proof
Oils and Incenses: Violet, Rose and Geranium
Gemstones: Amethyst, Sapphire, Aventurine, Lapis Lazuli

***

Chakra #7 & associated color: Crown / White or deep Purple

Name meaning: Thousand - petal lotus
Quote: "The Divine is part of me and I am part of the Divine"
Symbolizes/ Focus: Spiritual mastery and transformation; the gateway to God; "lets go and lets God"; bliss, understanding, oneness with the Divine, peace, expanded consciousness, Communication with the Divine; do it as God would have it done
Sense: N/A
Endocrine gland: Pineal
Health/Healing: pineal, cerebral cortex, central nervous system and right eye
Location: Top of head
Element: Magentum
Age like personality: Ageless
To balance it: Visualize the Light dissolving all the cells of your body so that you are made of nothing but Divine Light. Stay as long as you can, then visualize your body recreating itself within the light. Pray.
Well balanced personality: the Guru; knowing that there is something more, knowing your true path and living your life accordingly; surrender to the divine will, being *one* with the Universe; Ego is replaced with the Universal Consciousness, Peace and fulfillment, enlightenment and bliss; senses life from a spiritual perspective

Out of balance personality: Ego-centered, controlling, arrogance, materialism
Oils and Incenses: Amber and Sandalwood
Gemstones: Clear Quartz, Amethyst, Diamond, white jade

**

How to scan each other's energy fields

Choose a partner and scan each other's chakras. Ask your partner to lie down supine, and start scanning each chakra, from crown to root, for about three minutes each. Keep your palms still a few inches above the body. You can also move your hands in circles a few inches above the body. You don't need to touch his/her body in order to feel the energy.

You may feel tingling, hot, cold, pressure, warmth, pain, or simply nothing. Feel the difference between the way each chakra feels and take notes.

When you are done, ask your partner to lie down prone and repeat the scanning of each chakra. See if you can sense any difference.

After you've scanned each other's energy fields, share your observations with each other. What did you feel while scanning? What did you feel when your partner scanned your energy fields?

**

The Reiki Symbols

Cho-Ku-Rei - physical healing - is the power symbol used to increase the power of Reiki. It means "put all the power of the Universe here." This symbol is also known as "the light switch." The light is switched on when you put your hands down to heal.

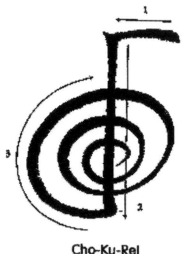

Cho-Ku-Rei
Physical Body
Increase power - "The Light Switch"

The physical healing Reiki symbol can be used:
- At the beginning of the session to increase the power.
- At the end of the session to seal in the healing energies.
- To clear a room of negative psychic energy and seal it in light, making it a sacred space.

- To protect yourself, your home (draw the symbols in the air on each wall, on your bed, on the album with photos of your beloved ones), your children, your pets or anything you value.
-To bless your food or cleanse your water before drinking.

***

Sei-He-Ki - emotional healing.
The emotional healing Reiki symbol can be used:
- To release emotional upsets and traumas.
- To heal relationship problems.
- To release spirit attachments.
- To heal addictions (actually addiction to any chemicals is the result of an addiction to the emotion generated by the usage of that particular chemical); addictions are strong forms of attachment.

Sei-He-Ki
Emotional Body
Emotional healing, purification, protection, and clearing

- To guard a space against negative emotions.
- To enhance the use of *affirmations*.
- To invoke protection and purification.
- To balance the right and left sides of the brain, bringing harmony and peace.

Note: My first esoteric teacher, Mr. Alexandru E. Russu taught me *how to practice affirmations*: Stay comfortable and relaxed while saying aloud the affirmations. It is even more powerful to look into your own eyes in the mirror while saying them. It builds more confidence and generates more self-love.

Say each one 20 times aloud enough so that your ear will hear from the inside and from the outside. Feel the feeling of being that way, and visualize yourself acting upon being this way. Try to get rid of any other thoughts with calm and the acceptance that is normal to have other thoughts coming to you.

***

Hon-Sha-Ze-Sho-Nen - mental body healing and distant healing, the Akashic Records, Past, Present, Future.

The distant healing/mental body healing Reiki symbol can be used:
- For distance or absentee healing (and hands-on healing for yourself and others) – send to someone from across the room, across town, or even in other parts of the country or world.

- For better intuitive healing, psychic readings and mediumship, automatic writing sessions, etc – by entering into the *Akashic records*, the life records of each soul. (The Akashic records describe the karmic goals, debts, contracts and life purpose of each soul's many incarnations, including the present lifetime.)

Hon-She-Ze-Sho-Nen
Mental Body
Distance healing, the Akashic Records,
past-present-future

- For healing traumas from the past (from current life or past lives); past life patterns can be uncovered and released, and karmic debts resolved.
- For sending healing energy into the future, to be found when needed (a future surgery, meeting, etc)

***

Dai-Ko-Mayo - healing of the soul and the spiritual body; transmits the Reiki attunements.

The spiritual healing Reiki symbol can be used:
-To heal disease from its highest source, from its first cause. The spiritual body levels contain the blueprint or template from which the physical body is derived. Healing at this level makes for profound changes, the type commonly labeled miracles.
-To create a healer, in the process of passing Reiki attunements.

Use all these Reiki symbols in any Reiki session. Keep it simple and powerful. You don't have the time or enough knowledge to analyze and decide what symbols need to be used. By using all of them, you allow miracles to happen, you allow the Spirit world to work through you for the highest good of the receiver.

***

Raku - brings Enlightenment and releases us from the illusion of the material world. It grounds the consciousness level of enlightenment energy of Reiki, into the body of the healer.

Raku can be used:
-At the end of the attunement process, to disconnect the aura of the student and teacher
-In cases of clients with high levels of negative energy and diseases, just once at the end of the session, for the purpose of protection. Personally I also draw it once at the end of distant healing sessions, especially if the receiver is very close to me emotionally—it helps the Reiki practitioner come back to here and now.

Activating Reiki symbols:
The symbols can be drawn using your fire finger (next to the index finger), or imagine a beam of light coming out of the palm chakra and draw them by moving the flattened hand in the air.
You can draw the symbols in the air in front of you.
You can draw the symbols on your palms before the session.
You can also draw the symbols on your body.
You can also visualize the symbol or imagine yourself drawing it. Any of these ways will activate Reiki symbols. The important thing is your intention: intend to activate the symbol and it will activate. The above methods are simply ways of expressing your intention.

***

How to attune your pendulum and how to scan the energy fields using it

Hold the pendulum between your hands and watch each Reiki symbol for five minutes; then ask the pendulum "show me yes" (most of the time, "yes" is a clockwise motion) "show me no" (most of the time, "no" is a counter-clockwise motion). "Do you want to work with me in my Reiki sessions?"
Before using it, set the intention. It is imperative that you precede your question session with a prayerful request or statement.
Example: "It is my intention to receive truthful answers which will serve the good of all concerned."

Make sure to stop any pendulum motions between questions to clean any lingering energies that pertain to the previous question.

Hold the pendulum over the chakra and ask "Is this chakra open?" Be sure that the pendulum is as close to the body as possible without touching it.

"Yes" movement over a chakra means that the flow through that chakra is well balanced and full in that person's life.

"No" movement indicates the chakra closed, the energy is blocked, not in balance, and probably the person has negative experiences associated with it.

The size of the circle made by the pendulum is related to the chakra's strength and the amount of energy flowing through it. A large circle indicates a lot of energy flowing through it. If the circle is small, there is less energy flowing through it.

A completely still pendulum indicates either the chakra is reversing its spin, or the individual has so overused or held down and blocked the chakra that there is no energy involved.

***

A Reiki session in detail

-Get ready – center, wash hands, ground, draw Reiki symbols on your hands; set your intent (I would say: "Reiki Guides, please use me as an instrument for healing, please channel Life Force Energy through me for the highest good of 'Name'")

-Prepare the space (do Reiki symbols on the walls, on the table; sage or incense are great but make sure the client likes it)

-Put gem stones under the table (one for each major chakra)

-If the client experiences Reiki for the first time, explain how the session is going to go, what Reiki is and what do you represent—I always tell people that I am a tool in God' hands, a messenger, a channel for Life Force Energy, and that I don't give from me but through me.

-Give the client a stone to hold in their hand (ask them to pick one or hold their favorite stone)

-Swipe their aura from head to feet with a feather (you can put some aura cleansing or aromatherapy oils on the feather). Do it with fast movements.

-Use the pendulum (your personal one, attuned to Reiki) to identify if chakras are open or not. Holding the pendulum above each chakra, ask "is this chakra open?" the larger the circle, the more open it is.

-If you have a Kyanite crystal, hold it in your hand and, from head to feet, do circles, slow, with same speed from beginning to end, four inches above the body—this will open the chakra;

-Scan each chakra and give the Reiki session (2-3 min above each of the major chakra; then a little bit for the shoulders, elbows, wrists, hands, hips, knees, ankles and feet); you can stay longer in the area where you feel something different. You can also tell the client that you feel *something different* there and ask for feedback (it's the best way to say it). You can also use a crystal to direct energy to that spot

-Send Reiki from crown to feet (holding hands above the crown, with your intent)

-Step back and beam energy into their aura—you can use a crystal if you want

-Draw Cho-Ku-Rei to seal the Reiki energy (you can draw a big symbol over them from head to root

-If you want to give them a short term attunement, do Dai-Ko-Mayo on them
-You can put any symbol in any chakra of someone—it will stay there for 21 days
-Swipe their aura with a feather
-Step back and do Raku (only once) between yourself and the client—make sure you don't do it at the level of their crown; this will disconnect you from the client's aura
-Use Raku at the end of all sessions (hands on or distant healing)—only once
-Let the client rest
-When the client is ready to stand up, offer a glass of water; exchange feedback. Tell them about the 21 days of cleansing (short term attunement)....

***

Methods of protection for you during and after giving a Reiki session

-Before the session, set your intent, to be detached emotionally from your client; it is *a must* to be emotionally detached during the session; this is a challenge, and a very important step we need to learn as healers. It is not easy when treating a beloved person, but keep in mind that you will be way more efficient when detached.
-If your client is very sick and you feel uncomfortable and disturbed by the negative energy, you can also set your intent to close your chakras at the minimum and just channel energy.

-During the session, if you feel pain in your hands or impatience or anxiety, shake your hands toward the floor and visualize dropping the negative energy in a bucket filled with *love*, where all negative energy is dissolved; I visualize *love* as being a white fluid, like the water of a waterfall, or like the light coming down between the branches of a tree.

-At the end of the session do Raku to disconnect your auras

-Wash hands and if you feel it's necessary keep them under the flowing water up to the elbows for a few minutes

-You can also go outside and ground—stand on the grass and do the tree exercise. If there is a tree, you can also hug the tree and visualize how all negative energy is taken deep down into the ground by the roots of the tree. Then, visualize how the roots are bringing up the clear, life-giving waters from the ground, and you are filling your body with this pure water as the tree does the same.

-You can run the "Cleansing Healing Thought Form" attunement: visualize a spiral of light coming through you, moving clockwise, from above your head down to your feet, as you breathe in; then, imagine a circle of light around, moving counterclockwise, as you breathe out, and visualize how all negative energy is getting out of your system; breathe in—breathe out; breathe in—breathe out; breathe in—breathe out

Use as many of these methods as you feel are necessary from case to case. However, we should always wash hands before and after any Reiki session.

***

How to pass a Reiki attunement

To make the description of passing a Reiki attunement easier, I'll give short names to the five Reiki symbols as follows:
1=Cho-Ku-Rei resonates strongest with the physical body level.
2=Sei-He-Ki with the emotional body.
3=Hon-Sha-Ze-Sho-Nen with the mental body.
4=Dai-Ko-Mayo works on the spiritual body level and transmits the Reiki attunements.
5=Raku - used at the end of the attunement process, or to disconnect from client at the end of a Reiki Session, hands on or distant.

The Reiki Attunement:
Behind the student – part 1:
1. Stand behind the student's chair. Center yourself and invite in the Reiki guides. Listen, feel, sense, open yourself, wait for the Reiki guides to come into you and surround you. When you are ready—you will be guided to begin.
2. Place both hands over the student's head, hold until you feel the crown chakra is ready to be opened. Then slowly open your hands as if you are seeing the crown chakra open as you go along. Then turn your hands with palms up to invite the Reiki energy in.
3. Blow over the crown chakra to awaken and cleanse it. With your right hand over the head, draw on the student's head the **1, 2, 3, 4**. Blow again on the crown chakra. Blowing is also a way of breathing life into this newly opened chakra.

In front of the student:
4. Move around to the front of the student and take their hands in yours and move them up to a

193

comfortable height for you. Wrap your left hand around the student's hands with her fingers just below your hand. Touch each of the tips of her fingers with love, then with your right hand draw *all four symbols* over her/his hands. Then clasp the student's hands between both of yours, point her fingers down, and blow open her hands starting from the wrist to the fingers.

5.Open the student's hands and keeping her hands at the heart chakra level on her knees, draw **1** on her palms, then hit her palms three times (this wakes up the palms and imprints the symbols on the palms). Repeat this after the **2**, **3** and **4**.

6.Then place your hands over theirs for soothing.

7.Move your intention to her feet. Keep your left hand on her hand and with your right hand, draw **1,2,3,4** on the right foot, then **1,2,3,4** on the left foot.

8.Rub student's hands—palm to palm—then swipe away and move your hands behind you.

9.Stand in front of the student and blow from the root to the crown chakra. Then raise your left hand, palm up, to bring in all the love and power from the Universe. With your right hand, palm facing student, draw **1,2,3,4** again. This opens the student's chakras.

Behind the student – part2:

10.Move to the back of the chair to close and protect the student's aura. Start from the student's lower left shoulder, draw **1**. Move a little higher on the shoulder and draw **2**. <u>Do not close the Crown chakra.</u> Move to the top right shoulder and draw **3**. Lower on the shoulder draw the **4**.

11.Step back and draw the Raku down the student's spine, from the shoulders to ground. Do this three times. You will feel a shift in your own energy and the student's with the Raku. This will release your connection to the student.

12.Step back and "look" at the student, her aura, her energy, etc. Ask the Reiki guides if everything is as it should be. When you sense the attunement is completed, go around to the front of the student and welcome her with open arms. The attunement is finished.

Reiki Teachers, please respect your bodies. Giving too many Reiki attunements at once can produce damages to the nervous system. It is empowering, but the energy can be overwhelming. As you start to pass on Reiki attunements, do it gradually. Start with one attunement, then two, four, etc. Listen to your body—it will know when to stop. If you have a big class, take breaks between every few attunements and ground yourself.

Thank you for serving humanity! Be blessed!

***

Gifts from Stellar Beings, channeled by Shaman Manin

These are only the most common three Energetic Expansion Attunements that have been used successfully in my Reiki practice and incorporated in my Reiki classes. There are many more gifts from the Universe available to you, through the teachings of Shaman Manin (http://veinsofsilver.org).

Cleansing-Healing Thought Form Attunement

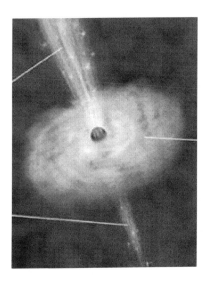

Look at the image above and breathe in and out three times, inhaling light spiraling through the top of your head, clockwise, and exhaling all stress and negativity in the opposite direction.

Quan Yin Cubed Attunement

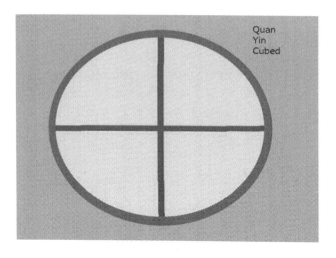

Look at the photo above, and placing your right hand on your heart, say:
I am running the Quan-Yin-Cubed Attunement on my heart
For *grace, compassion, mercy, forgiveness* and *peace*

Shaman Manin says:

I love myself. I forgive myself. I am at peace with myself.

I love you, I forgive you. I am at peace with you. Aho.

(*Note: "You" meaning anyone*)
And we can go further and say:
**I love the whole world.
I forgive everyone who has hurt me in the past.
I am at peace with *all that is*.**

Identify with your higher self when you say "I love myself." Imagine the Divine in front of you. This way, you will know if your intentions, thoughts and actions are ego based or soul based.

"I am *one* with my higher self" is a good affirmation to start with.

*

Flood Light Attunement

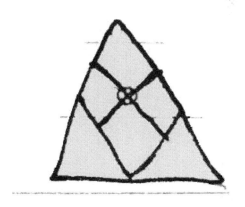

Look at the yellow triangle, representing the Flood Light Attunement, and say
Run Flood Light!
Imagine that you are filling your solar plexus with golden yellow light. Feel the nurturing and empowering energy.

About the author

Laura O'Neale is a Reiki Master/Teacher, Certified Massage Therapist and Meditation Techniques Guide. Her soul mission is to heal and teach through spiritual love. She knows that we are all beloved children of the Universe, and she has been called to assist the seekers toward their happiness.

Laura earned a Bachelors Degree in Computer Science in Romania, her home country. Currently, she resides in Washington, D.C. However, she considers herself a universal soul, because people around the world have a home in her heart.

Please visit Laura at www.YourLightWithin.com

For events, classes or other services provided by Laura,
or to purchase online Laura's books, please visit
www.YourLightWithin.com

Laura's books:

The Journey of the Colorful Stars
A Pathway toward Love, Faith and Healing

&

Reiki and the Path to Enlightenment
A Reiki and Shamanic Journal for Energy
Healing Students, Practitioners and Teachers

&

Focused on Spirit
A Journal about Spiritual Gifts Serving
Humanity

Made in the USA
Charleston, SC
07 April 2012